As seen on
Today and *Live with Regis and Kelly*

Praise for the Queen of Clean®!

"Linda Cobb, the self-styled Queen of Clean®, sweeps into the big time with spotless timing for a book on dirt.... *Talking Dirty with the Queen of Clean®* ... has certainly cleaned up."

—*People*

"There's no stain Linda Cobb can't tame."

—*New York Post*

"Let's face it, cleanup problems are a stain on all of us, but since the Queen has been on the show, we have all become sponges, soaking up every drop of information she has."

—Dan Davis, *Good Morning Arizona*, KTVK-TV, Phoenix

"There isn't any stain or cleaning problem for which Cobb doesn't have a solution. ..."

—*The Arizona Republic*

"Her enthusiasm is contagious, and her cleaning tips are both effective and fun. When Linda talks dirty everybody listens. She truly is the Queen of Clean®."

—Joe Daily, morning show host, WRNQ Radio, New York

"The Queen of Clean® is one of the most popular guests we've ever had. After all, have you ever met someone who uses things like Tang™, lemon juice, and Massengill™ to clean? Neither have we. All hail the Queen of Clean!®"

—*Beth and Bill in the Morning*, KESZ 99.9 FM Radio, Phoenix

You, too, can conquer clutter!

Also by Linda Cobb

How the Queen Cleans Everything
A Queen for All Seasons
The Royal Guide to Spot and Stain Removal
Talking Dirty Laundry with the Queen of Clean®
Talking Dirty with the Queen of Clean®

The
Queen
of
Clean®
Conquers Clutter

Linda Cobb

POCKET BOOKS

New York London Toronto Sydney Singapore

An *Original* Publication of POCKET BOOKS

 POCKET BOOKS, a division of Simon & Schuster, Inc.
1230 Avenue of the Americas, New York, NY 10020

ISBN: 0-7434-2832-3

First Pocket Books trade paperback printing December 2002

10 9 8 7 6 5 4 3 2 1

For information regarding special discounts for bulk purchases,
please contact Simon & Schuster Special Sales at 1-800-456-6798
or business@simonandschuster.com

Book design by Jaime Putorti

Printed in the U.S.A.

This book is dedicated to my friends and fans in
Arizona, where it all started.
You made me the Queen of Clean.
Because of all of you, it's good to be Queen.

Acknowledgments

Special thanks to everyone at KTVK-TV's *Good Morning Arizona*, where it all began.

Beth McDonald, and Bill Austin, hosts of *Beth and Bill in the Morning*, KESZ Radio, Phoenix, AZ. You have been with me every step of the way and I have learned so much from you about radio, integrity, and kindness.

Louise Burke, Publisher at Pocket Books. Thank you for your tireless dedication to quality.

Brenda Copeland, editor and friend. Thank you for ridding my manuscript of clutter.

Jaime Putorti, Carole Schwindeller, Cathy Gruhn, Marisa Stella, Barry Porter, and everyone at Pocket Books. Your efforts make me look so good.

Duane Dooling. Your friendship is a treasure.

Claire Bush, for your invaluable help in putting this book together.

Special friends Brian Gilbert, Norman Clark, Jim Ranaldo, Lisa and Bobby Aguilar, Betty Archambeau, Peggy

Barker, Alan Centofante, Catherine Holland, and all our neighbors who put up with camera crews and satellite trucks at all hours of the day and night.

Dr. Kevin Mueller and staff. Thanks for the smile!

Win and Carolyn Holden, partners, but more important, friends.

Last, but most important, I thank my family. The Queen Mother, who is also my best friend; husband John, The King, who is with me each step of the way; and our combined family: David and Janette; Victoria; Pat and Laura, John, Justin, April and Desmond; Nanette, David and Patrick; Nancy, Doug, Drew, Ashley and Lilly Ann. Cousin, Charlene Staub. The Pussycat Princess, Zoey, for providing research material. Without the love and support of all of you, there would be no joy in the palace.

To all of you who are reading this, I thank you for Conquering Clutter with the Queen of Clean®.

Contents

Contents

A place for everything and everything in its place. Who hasn't heard that phrase? And who hasn't thought of it as a fantasy? No one has clutter in their fantasy, but in reality, everyone does. Let's face it: No matter how big your home or how much storage space you have, clutter always seems to have a life of its own, abiding by that law of physics that says matter expands to fill the space available. If you have to stop to clear a work area every time you start to carry out a task like cleaning, cooking, or laundry; if you're constantly losing your keys and you have to wade through eighteen months of unread *Reader's Digest*s to get to the *TV Guide;* then you have a clutter problem. But in case you think clutter is just an aggravation, consider this: Clutter is costly! Have you ever:

• Paid late fees on a bill because you misplaced it until it was too late? Those credit card bills are high enough without tacking on late fees.

- Bought duplicates of the same item without knowing it? Okay, it's nice to stock up on lightbulbs, but twelve boxes?

- Forked over unnecessary fines at the library or video store? Sure, *Caddyshack* may have given you a lot of laughs, but forget to return the tape on time and that $8 fine will do a lot to wipe the smile off your face.

Mistakes happen, but habitual disorganization can lead to more than your fair share of unhappy consequences. Consider a good friend of mine who carefully arranged every detail of her wedding—but forgot to bring the key to the reception hall for the caterers. While the food and supplies were being unloaded on the sidewalk, the frantic bride had to dispatch a friend to her home for the missing key. The unlucky caterers had to hastily set up the wedding feast while the ceremony was taking place. Not an auspicious beginning to a lifetime union. Then there was the mother who baked and iced two dozen cupcakes for her son's class birthday party—and left them on the kitchen counter in a last-minute dash to get out the door on time. And what about the health care executive whose closet was so hopelessly disorganized that he once attended an important meeting wearing one black and one brown shoe! Do any of these stories sound familiar? Situations like these are upsetting and stressful, but you'll be happy to know they're also unnecessary—a little less clutter and a little more organization is all it takes.

You know, the reasons for holding on to clutter are as many and varied as clutter itself. Often we are loath to get rid of a particular item because we think it might come in handy "sometime" or "somewhere." We hold on to broken goods, thinking that the day will come when we'll have the time or the know-how to repair them or scavenge the parts to repair something else. We keep possessions because they have sentimental value, or because they hold promises that we aren't willing to part with. I have a friend whose shelves are full of good intentions: Tae Bo™ tapes that were going to transform her into a feisty size 6, a French language course for a trip that never materialized, a basket full of wool that one day hopes to become a sweater. Is that you? It doesn't have to be.

We all have our favorite things that we don't want to part with. That's fine. Nobody but the most strident organizational fiend would suggest that you get rid of all your sentimental favorites in your clutter clear out. And yet, what happens when everything is a sentimental favorite, when you're so crowded by things from the past that you don't have room for the present? Memories are great—until you have to dust them.

I'm going to let you in on a trade secret. You *can* get out from all that clutter. You can live a life that's more organized and, consequently, less stressful. And you don't have to spend money to do it. The key to getting out from under all that clutter and getting organized is not a matter of adding anything: it's the thoughtful elimination of time- and space-wasting things. In most cases, you don't need to buy a single new product to get yourself organized; you can use what you've already got to control the clutter monster in your life—and keep it tamed.

You already have what it takes to conquer clutter and get organized. So let's work together to get it done. It's easier than you think!

CHAPTER I

Twenty
Questions

*E*nquiring minds want to know, right? I'm a Queen with a mission—to help you find out what will work best to keep your life clutter-free and organized. Just go down this list and answer these twenty questions. And be honest. We don't give out demerits. This isn't about *right* and *wrong*. It's about identifying your strong points—knowing what you're good at, what you have a knack for—as well as finding out where you need to improve your clutter-containing skills. Just remember: No matter how big your home, the biggest room is usually room for improvement!

1. Are you constantly running late?
   ❏ Never ❏ Sometimes ❏ Often

2. Do you have trouble letting go of objects that have long outlived their use?
   ❏ Never ❏ Sometimes ❏ Often

3. Are you using eyeliner and lipstick to write down messages because you can't seem to find a pencil or pen in your drawers?
   ❏ Never   ❏ Sometimes   ❏ Often

4. During the last six months, have you had to search for your car keys . . .
   ❏ Never   ❏ Sometimes   ❏ Often

5. Do you organize and reorganize, but always end up with the same amount of stuff?
   ❏ Never   ❏ Sometimes   ❏ Often

6. Have you ever run the baby's formula through the automatic coffee maker because the microwave is used for storage and you couldn't find a pan?
   ❏ Never   ❏ Sometimes   ❏ Often

7. Have you ever missed a doctor appointment or social engagement because you just plain "forgot" all about it?
   ❏ Never   ❏ Sometimes   ❏ Often

8. Is your closet filled to the rafters with clothing and shoes? Does it contain clothes of all sizes?
   ❏ Never   ❏ Sometimes   ❏ Often

9. How many times during the past year have you given unneeded items to charity?
   ❏ Never   ❏ Sometimes   ❏ Often

10. Have you ever tucked in a pile of clothes because there is so much stuff on the bed you can't tell if your child is in there or not?
    ❏ Never   ❏ Sometimes   ❏ Often

11. Have you ever found an item you needed—after you'd purchased its replacement?
    ❏ Never ❏ Sometimes ❏ Often

12. Do the kids think that everybody turns their underwear inside out on Tuesday, Thursday, and Saturday to get an extra day's wear out of it?
    ❏ Never ❏ Sometimes ❏ Often

13. Are there papers on your desk that you haven't looked through for over a month?
    ❏ Never ❏ Sometimes ❏ Often

14. Do your neighbors come to your house first every time there is a scavenger hunt?
    ❏ Never ❏ Sometimes ❏ Often

15. When you start cleaning and organizing your house, do you tend to get sidetracked and start another project?
    ❏ Never ❏ Sometimes ❏ Often

16. Do you generally know what time it is, or do you usually need to consult your watch?
    ❏ Never ❏ Sometimes ❏ Often

17. Is your idea of clearing off the countertop sliding everything off it into the wastebasket or drawer?
    ❏ Never ❏ Sometimes ❏ Often

18. Does your car sit outside because you need your garage for storage?
    ❏ Never ❏ Sometimes ❏ Often

19. Are you able to shut all of your dresser drawers without clothes hanging out the sides?
    ❑ Never   ❑ Sometimes   ❑ Often

20. Do you have to remove dirty pots and pans from your oven before you can use it?
    ❑ Never   ❑ Sometimes   ❑ Often

Now it's time to check your responses. For each time you answered NEVER, give yourself 1 point. For each SOME-TIMES answer, give yourself 2 points, and give yourself 3 points for each time you answered OFTEN. Now add up your score and let's see how you did.

If you scored 20 to 35 points, you are indeed a royal organizer. Good for you! Use this book to help you hone your best organizing instincts and make yourself the Queen of your own castle. You probably have a lot of the basics in use, so now's the time to pay attention to the small organizing details you may previously have overlooked. Fine-tune your storage systems and banish clutter once and for all, and make sure you are spending enough time on evaluating and eliminating.

If you scored 36 to 45 points, you fit into the largest group of clutter conquerors. Constantly trying to improve, you nevertheless feel like you are running on a treadmill as the clutter continues to grow ... and grow. ... You're not part of the remedial organizing group (see the next paragraph), but you still have a ways to go to get your palace organized and clutter-free. Why don't you start with the chapters that pertain to your biggest problems? You'll make great strides if you really question and take stock of the areas you want to conquer—find out what's not working before you come up with solutions. Take it in small stages and work through your clutter crisis area by area.

If you scored 46 to 60 points, then, yes, let's just say it—*you have a clutter problem. A BIG ONE!* But we're not going to lock you in the dungeon and throw away the key (there probably wouldn't be room for you, anyway). Chances are you look at the clutter accumulating around you and feel defeated before you begin, and so haven't begun. Until now. Let me walk you through this book. Select a small area to start your clutter busting so that you can step back and appreciate your efforts almost immediately. Once you begin and get a feel for conquering clutter (even in the smallest way), you'll begin to believe in order again. Remember, it took time to collect all of that clutter, so it will take time to remove it. Read on to elevate your royal status in your home and eliminate some of the stress that you deal with every day. And don't get discouraged. Rome wasn't organized in a day!

CHAPTER 2

Getting Started

*A*re you a Harried Harriet? Harriet unlocks the front door with a heavy heart. It's past dinnertime already. An unexpected phone call and a long line at the supermarket have made her late—again. Dodging a lone sock in the hallway (how did that get there?), she can hear the answering machine go off: "Mom! Pick up! I'm waiting for a ride at soccer practice!" Harriet slides her bags full of groceries onto the kitchen counter, where the movie the family watched last night still sits patiently waiting. Darn, she meant to return that to the video store. That's another $3 in fines. The dog has chewed a slipper again. His leash has been missing since yesterday, and no one has been able to take him for a much needed walk. Harriet is—well, harried! She's tired, hungry, and frustrated. Dinner's not made, and the house is a mess. Does this sound like the end of your average workday?

Life is becoming increasingly complex. Spending time at home should be a relaxing, fun experience, not an exercise in frustration. There is an easier way to live than Harriet's daily routine. Wouldn't it be much nicer to come home like Peaceful Pauline? Pauline opens the front door, placing her keys in the basket on the hall table and her handbag on a handy wall hook nearby—right next to the dog's leash! Tonight's dinner is already cooked and ready to be popped into the oven. Last week, Pauline cooked a double batch of spaghetti and froze the second half for another day. That leaves half an hour to change clothes and read and sort the mail before it's time to eat. After dinner, the kids can take the dog for a walk. This evening, the family will watch a video together, and Pauline might even have time to call her mother for a chat. No wonder Pauline is peaceful!

What's the difference between feeling like a Harried Harriet and a Peaceful Pauline? It comes down to this: clutter control and organization. Controlling clutter and organizing your life may seem like an impossible task, but just think of all the impossible tasks that you do every day. And think how much easier they would be if you weren't surrounded by clutter and chaos! Conquering clutter really does pay off—in fact, conquering clutter has such terrific benefits that once you begin, you'll soon become hooked. If you've gotten used to living in clutter and chaos, you'll be pleasantly surprised to find how enjoyable conquering clutter and getting organized can be. You can relax in your own home, find things when you need them, enjoy your day-to-day activities, and feel in control of your life. And, if you're like most of us in these days of instant gratification, take heart: conquering clutter pays off immediately!

I once had a fortune cookie that read: "Every journey, no matter how long, begins with a single step." What is the first step in getting organized? Having a system, of course. A workable solution for daily life that really gets results. And that's where I come in! I've worked up a little system so that you can take me with you from room to room, so you can let me—the *QUEEN*—be your guide! It's a little reminder to help you follow through with your clutter-busting intentions, to keep you from getting distracted or feeling defeated before you begin. Give it (me!) a try.

*Q*uestion

*U*npack

*E*valuate

*E*liminate

*N*eaten up!

*Q*uestion. What is the purpose of this room, cupboard, drawer? What do I see that doesn't work here? How can I make better use of this space? Why am I keeping this article of clothing? What am I happy with? What works here and what doesn't? If the twins are teenagers, why do we still have two shelves of Dr. Seuss books on display? If the summer sun is shining, why do we have four mismatched mittens on the table in the hall?

*U*npack. Get it all out in the open, one thing at a time. For example, if you're working in a closet, do only the shoes first. Sort through one shelf in the linen closet. Remove the contents of one drawer in the kitchen. Remember, only by taking things out will you really have a sense of what you have and what you need to do with it. You can't conquer clutter if you can't see it.

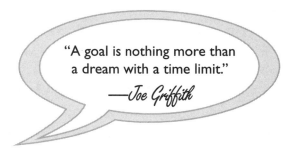

"A goal is nothing more than a dream with a time limit."

—*Joe Griffith*

*E*valuate. It's judgment day. Ask some questions: When was the last time I used this? Do I really need this? If so, is this where the item should be? Then prepare to stash it or trash it. Okay, I know, this is the hard part. If your heart is saying you need it and your mind says it hasn't been used since Nixon was president, sometimes it's hard to be impartial. Look at things as if you were helping a friend. If the things weren't your possessions, what would you do? Then do it.

*E*liminate. One bag is for the neighbor, a charity, or the school fund-raiser. The other bag is headed straight for the trash. Every item that isn't destined to go back into that drawer, closet, or shelf belongs to one of these two bags. Get rid of the excuses for keeping things while you're at it. I've heard them all: *I might need that someday. Aunt Margaret gave me that. Somebody might be able to make use of that, so I'll hang on to it.* Eliminate your excuses as you eliminate your excess stuff. They're both clutter, and you'll live better without them.

*N*eaten Up. This is the fun part. Oh, how clever you'll feel as you admire your rows of neatly organized shoes, freshly straightened spices, or tidy stacks of towels. This is the time you get to put things where you want them and stand back and admire your work. Don't be afraid to be unconventional. If you like storing your underwear rolled in clear hanging racks on the back of the bedroom door, that's fine, as long as it works for you. Try things out, and change them if they don't work the way you hoped they would.

So, now that you have a system, what's the best way to use it? Start small. I'd like to suggest that you devote just 15 minutes at a time to this process—that's all it takes to really get results. If you like, you can even use your kitchen timer to remind you—or release you, if you're really resisting the idea. So often we feel discouraged because a task seems overwhelming. This simple 15-minute rule lets you off the hook. You don't have to eliminate your clutter all in one day. You can chip at it over time. Believe me, I've tried many ways to manage my day-to-day life, and this is the only one that works consistently. Don't be surprised if your 15 minutes slip away before you realize it! Then, if you like, you can reset the timer for another 15 minutes and tackle another drawer, shelf, closet, or box. It's up to you! You never realized organizing could actually be fun, did you? C'mon. Let's get started!

CHAPTER 3

You Can Take It with You

Making Cents of Your Wallet

I told you we were going to start small! Let's begin by tackling that wallet—you know, the one that still holds your high school library card and the ticket stubs from your senior prom... (Not to mention the shoe rental receipt from your bowling league that ended in 1994, and the unlucky lottery ticket from last year's big draw.) Don't fret. Ten minutes is all it takes—if you take the *QUEEN* with you, that is.

*N*ot only will organizing your wallet get you started on your clutter busting—and make you feel more organized almost instantly—it may even improve your health! Men can actually develop back and hip problems from sitting on that bulging wallet; women may find their wallet is the heaviest thing in their purse next to the cosmetic bag. And heavy purses can mean sore shoulders.

*Q*uestion: *What do I want from this space? A streamlined wallet in which I can find things when I need them, a wallet that doesn't bulge or pop open unexpectedly.*

*U*npack: Pull out your wallet, take a seat at a table or desk, and get ready to de-clutter. Empty your wallet. Remove everything—yes, money too!

*E*valuate: Now put the contents of your wallet into three piles. One pile should contain discards, the things you are *really* going to throw out this time, such as the photo that "made you look skinny" in 1992. One stack will hold items to be put away or stored somewhere else. These are things like your original social security card, original birth certificate, and the directions for your personal organizer. (If you don't know how it works now, you never will.) The last grouping will contain the things you *really* need and will return to your wallet. These are items such as your driver's license, credit cards, organ donor card, emergency medical information, and the all-important money!

*E*liminate: Once you have finished sorting, go through the items you'll be discarding one last time, to be sure you aren't throwing out anything you should keep. Don't discard receipts from items you may still want to return, or might need for warranty information, for instance. These items need to be filed. Phone numbers you've jotted down should be transferred to your address book, and business cards should be put away in a Rolodex® or other appropriate place. Now is the time to get the scissors and cut up expired or unwanted credit cards too. Cut them or shred them so that the number is not readable. You might even want to mix the pieces up in separate trash baskets. Remember, even though your old card is expired, the number on the new one is the same with a new expiration date.

*N*eaten Up: Now take some time to reorganize your wallet. Think about how you use the things in your wallet and what you have to search for each time you want it. If you have a frequent-coffee-drinker card, and you use it each morning, put it where you can find it the minute you open your wallet. Organize your paper money by denomination and you will never give away a ten-dollar bill thinking it's a single. Tuck the seldom used items in the out-of-the-way pockets. Keep frequently used credit cards up front and make sure they are always tucked in well. If you carry emergency medical information, keep it in a prominent spot, perhaps a window area in the wallet.

A Word to the Wise

Don't keep valuable original papers such as social security cards or birth certificates in your wallet. The Social Security Administration recommends that you keep these documents with your valuable papers and bring them out only when required, such as when you get a new job or open a bank account. A lost or stolen social security card could create huge problems, so take a moment now to remove it and your birth certificate from your wallet. Take the time also to jot down the numbers of your credit cards, driver's license, and health insurance cards from your wallet or, better still, photocopy them on both sides. File this information in a safe place. Should your wallet get stolen, having this information at your fingertips will save you time and maybe even money.

If you've had the unfortunate experience of losing a wallet, then you already know the importance of canceling your credit cards, but there's more: call the three national credit-reporting organizations to place an immediate fraud alert on your name and social security number. A fraud alert means that you must be contacted by phone before any new charges can be made on your credit cards. No contact, no charges— simple! In addition, a call to the Social Security Fraud Line ensures that your social security number cannot be used to forge new documents or for any other fraudulent purpose. The numbers you need are:

Equifax® 1–888–766–0008

Experian® (formerly TRW) 1–888–397–3742

Trans Union™ 1–800–680–7289

Social Security Administration Fraud Line
1–800–269–0271

Loosen Those Purse Strings

Any man who has ever heard the words "Can you hold my purse for a minute, dear?" knows how heavy a woman's handbag can be. Many women use shoulder bags that are so heavy that carrying around these "mini-suitcases" leads to neck and shoulder pain. Keeping purses as light and clutter-free as possible can eliminate many aches and pains! Ladies, now it's time to organize those purses.

Again, empty everything out on a counter, desk, or worktable. Next, unpack, sorting out the obvious junk (used tissues, fuzzy Life Savers, gum without wrappers, and that Christmas card from two years ago), and discard. Now we'll work with what's left. Rescue the necessary items, such as your wallet, keys, cosmetic bag, cell phone, and appointment book, and set aside. It's time to evaluate and eliminate the rest of the items. Think "lighten up"—your neck and shoulders will thank you for this!

You should need only one cosmetic bag. Try using a light-colored one: it will be easier to find inside the dark interior of your purse. Empty out your cosmetic bag, and give the inside a quick wipe-down using a clean cloth or damp paper towel moistened with your favorite dish soap. Wipe dry, and replace only the cosmetics you really use. Be ruthless here: one lipstick, a compact, some eyedrops if you use them, a spare mascara and eyeshadow, should be all you need. Discard any broken or old tubes of makeup, keeping in mind that cosmetics manufacturers recommend replacing your eye makeup at least every six months to lessen the risk of infection to delicate eye tissue.

Turn your purse inside out or hold it upside down, and give it a good shake. Wipe out the interior with a clean, soft cloth. Revitalize your leather handbag by running a damp cloth over a bar of moisturizing facial soap (such as Dove®), then wiping down your purse; no need to rinse. Patent leather bags will shine like new if you rub a little petroleum jelly into the surface and buff with a soft cloth. Vinyl purses can be cleaned with a damp cloth and a little dishwashing soap, then wiped dry. Remove stubborn scuff marks from vinyl with lighter fluid, taking care to dispose of the rag or paper towels outside. Now for the fun part. When your purse is clean and dry, neaten up by returning your wallet, cosmetic bag, keys, and other necessary items. If you have a purse with different compartments, try keeping each item in the same place so you can simply reach for things rather than hunting for them. It helps when you are feeling for something you need. (I always keep my wallet on the left side of my purse and my cosmetic bag on the right.)

Backpack—Or Pack Mule?

If you feel like a pack mule every time you shoulder your backpack, it's time to lighten up. Serious hikers know that the maximum weight to be carried in a backpack is 38 pounds— and that's for a three-day hike, folks! Anything more can cause back and neck injuries. Lest you scoff at this figure, step over to the bathroom scale and weigh your pack. You may be amazed at what you've been toting around. Parents, in particular, should take care that kids empty their backpacks regularly. Those schoolbooks are heavy, and excess weight on the back is not good for growing strong, healthy spines.

Again, you'll want to empty your backpack and examine the contents. Get rid of old papers, leaky pens, that leftover peanut-butter-and-jelly sandwich, and empty water bottles. If you reuse your water bottles, fill them with warm water and add one teaspoon or so of baking soda. Put the lid on and shake well to clean the bottle. Make sure you wipe the neck of the bottle well with a damp cloth and baking soda, and then rinse well, refill, and put in the refrigerator. Water bottles do need to be cleaned regularly, and using baking

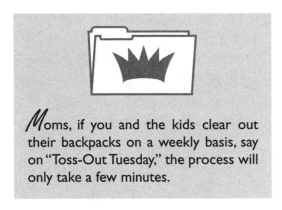

*M*oms, if you and the kids clear out their backpacks on a weekly basis, say on "Toss-Out Tuesday," the process will only take a few minutes.

soda instead of dish soap will eliminate that soapy taste in your water. Arrange books and folders in one stack, personal items like headphones, water bottles, cell phones, and cosmetic bags in another. Wipe down the inside of the backpack with a clean, damp cloth and let dry. Return books, papers and personal items to the pack, and keep like items grouped together: books, folders, papers, and tape in one pocket; headphones, cell phones, and spare batteries in another; lunch bag and water bottle kept separately. You can't always have everything in an exact place, but at least you'll know what's in each pocket without searching through all of them.

Now step back and admire your work. Almost makes you want to go back to school, doesn't it?

A Brief Word About Briefcases

Do you use a briefcase? Then follow these steps for de-cluttering your "office away from the office." Again, start on a flat surface and remove everything. Discard obvious clutter such as sandwich wrappers, junk mail, and last week's newspaper. Place receipts in one pile, files and papers in another, electronic equipment like laptops, headsets, and cell phones in a third. If you need receipts for business purposes, file them. Otherwise, toss them away. You can use ordinary legal-size envelopes for receipts, labeling them by month for easy reference. Use manila folders to organize your papers: they're cheap, neat, easy to label, and don't take up much space. Go through your folders, discarding outdated paperwork; then return everything to the inside of the briefcase. Again, group related items together and arrange the interior of your case the same way each time so that you can find files, pens, or paper clips without searching.

See, that wasn't so hard. A few minutes spent organizing the things you use each and every day is worth the time you'll save trying to find that elusive credit card or the receipts for this month's expense report.

CHAPTER 4

Enter at Your Own Risk

Is your entry hall so filled with day-to-day clutter that you can barely get through the room, let alone find anything in it? Do you sometimes feel that your front door should have a sign posted that says Enter at Your Own Risk? When you come home, do you have to wade through a pile of shoes, boots, backpacks, several empty coffee cups, and a week's worth of newspapers to get to the front closet? Whether up front or at the side of the house, entry halls are often very small spaces—and small spaces have a habit of attracting clutter. So let's continue with my "start small" approach and tackle the entry hall before you lose another umbrella—or goodness me, your youngest child.

Approach this task in 15-minute blocks of time. Do what you can in that period and then stop if you want to. Of course, if you are feeling so energized with all you've achieved and want to keep going, that's okay too.

The key to organizing the entryway is to assign a logical space for things that are used every day, then stick to it. This will get you out the door and on your way to school, work, or errands without searching for necessary items.

Welcome

Step outside (careful, don't lock yourself out) and walk up to the door. Is the front walk swept and clear of clutter? Can you see all seven letters on the WELCOME mat? If the entry looks clean and appealing, good for you! If not, grab a broom and give the front porch a good sweeping. While you're at it, pull down any cobwebs you see hanging around. Odds and ends like skateboards, dog dishes, or old newspapers should be picked up and tossed out, or assigned to their proper place. Take a moment now to mix up a bucket of warm water with a squirt of your favorite all-purpose cleaner to wash down the front door if it needs it. If your doormat has seen better days, consider replacing it. You can find inexpensive doormats in a variety of designs at discount stores. (Best not to get one that says "Smith" if your name is "Jones"—even if it is on sale!)

Do Come In!

Now step inside the entryway. Pick up everything that doesn't belong, and ask yourself honestly, "Do I really need this?" It pays to be ruthless. You don't want to just move objects from one area of your home to another. This just spreads clutter; it doesn't eliminate it.

*R*emember you can only stay organized once you accept that *Less is more.* Less clutter equals less cleaning time, less frustration, and more space and enjoyment for you and your family.

Do you have a hall table or stand? Great. Let's start with that. Empty out any drawers, and toss out mystery keys and other clutter. Restock with a working flashlight, a couple of candles and some matches, and a supply of spare change. A decorative basket on top of the stand can hold mail (incoming and outgoing). Don't have a hall stand? Visit a thrift store or yard sale and keep an open mind. Storage options show up in all sorts of unusual places. A friend of mine bought an old piano bench for a song to use as a hall table; the seat lifted up and was great for storage. There are no rules here, just your imagination.

If you live in a rainy area, an umbrella stand in the corner is a nice touch. Coatracks are handy too, not only for jackets and sweaters but for hanging purses and backpacks. Hooks are a great storage option, especially in households with kids and pets. Make sure when you install the hooks that you leave enough space for even heavy coats to hang freely. You'll want to assign each child his or her own hook, perhaps a different color for each child, and be sure they check this area before they leave for school each morning. Use this area to hang the dog's leash too.

Get into the Closet

Make the most of your hall closet. Keep it well lighted by installing a battery operated light, and add a full-length mirror on the inside of the door. This allows a last-minute check before you go out the door. The mirror will also add a feeling of spaciousness when you open the door for guests.

If you have children, design a kid-friendly storage space in the closet. There are several methods you can use for this— just be sure that your child's possessions are within easy reach.

- You can assign a shelf or a portion of a shelf for each child's backpack, library books, and school papers. Use colored tape or masking tape with colored markers to identify each child's shelf or area.

- Plastic storage cubes are another great option for children's things; each child gets his or her own colored cube for easy identification.

- Over-the-door hangers (the kind used for shoes) can also create more space for storage in a closet. Use clear ones so that you can see what's hiding in each pocket. Again, assign pockets for each child to hold papers, books, gym clothes, and sweaters.

- A mesh laundry bag hung on a hook is great for organizing kids' toys and such.

The hall closet is also a logical place to create an area for pets' supplies too. If Fido wears a sweater or has a special outdoor toy, store that close by. If you use a towel to wipe those wet and muddy doggy paws, store it there too. Pick up a cute decorative basket and attach it to the wall near the leash and keep all of the doggie extras in it. Just remember to leave room for guests' coats.

Departure Area

Organize a "departure area" for everyday things that you use each day, such as your purse, briefcase, backpack, keys, cellular phone, laptop computer, and anything else you'll need to attend to, such as videos or library books that need returning. Don't forget your sports bag for a pre- or post-office workout.

Another handy time-saver in the entryway is a family bulletin board. Create an area for this by using a corkboard for reminder notes such as, "Honey, pick up Patrick from soccer at 5:00" or "Brittany and Stephen, here's the money for your

I like to keep an empty laundry basket in my car trunk for those days when I have lots of things to transport; I load the car the night before, lock the trunk, and in the morning I'm ready to go!

field trip." (Of course, this will only work if you have children named Patrick, Brittany, and Stephen.) Consider dividing the board into a section for each family member with colored tape or ribbon. Don't use a chalk or white board for this purpose; the pens and chalk seem to disappear like magic, and it's frustrating to spend your time searching for something to write on the board with.

Toss-Out Tuesday

Once everything is organized, allow a few quick minutes once a week to sort out anything that doesn't belong. I've had success using a method I call Toss-Out Tuesday. This is the day of the week I spend an extra minute or two sorting through my jewelry box, makeup bag, car glove box—whatever I use on that day—for unneeded items. Staying organized this way doesn't seem like extra work, since I'm doing it as I go along, and if I feel overwhelmed during the week (who doesn't?), I can always do Toss-Out Tuesday even if it's Friday or Monday. Try it and see if Toss-Out Tuesday works for you!

CHAPTER 5

Room for Living

These days, houses can have family rooms, living rooms, and "great rooms." You may have one of these rooms, or (lucky you!) all three. Still, it doesn't really matter whether your main family living space is the size of a spare bedroom or as spacious as a garage; it doesn't really matter what you call this room; and it doesn't really matter how big it is either—clutter accumulates in large rooms just as easily as in small. And the same clutter-conquering principles apply.

It's All in the Family (Room)

Family rooms are just that—spaces for the whole clan to hang out. What these areas all have in common is that they're the one room (next to the kitchen) that's a magnet for the clutter that seems to collect on a day-to-day basis. You know, the newspapers, magazines, mail, books, videos, crafts, hobbies, toys, items clipped from the newspaper, even office work and homework. If there ever was a room that needed organization with a capital *O*, it's this one!

Make sure that the family room doesn't become a drop-off spot for what everyone carries home at the end of the day. Backpacks, briefcases, and purses need to make it to the family entry/exit staging area for the next day, while sporting goods should go back to their proper storage area after use. A friend who has a house full of children and a husband who is a sports fan finally hit on a sneaky way to keep her family room from being declared a hazardous area. She has a rule that the television doesn't get turned on until skateboards, soccer balls, empty food dishes, and other clutter are cleared out of the room and returned to their proper place. Now it's amazing how quickly the place gets picked up—especially before a big football game on TV!

The best way to reorganize your family room is to step into the room on an especially cluttered day, like the Tuesday after a holiday weekend. With paper and pencil in hand, first see what needs to be removed, what needs storage, and what needs to be relocated. Do you have a pile of toys in one corner? Are there videos strewn all over the top of the television set? Is there a ball of knitting tucked into a corner of the sofa, with one needle missing? Do empty ice-cream bowls and snack wrappers congregate on the coffee table? Determining where your clutter comes from will help you hone in on the source of the problem. Often by making some changes in other nearby rooms, you will gain some control of the family room.

What's on TV

Let's consider the television area, since this is often the focal point of the family room. Where is your VCR or DVD player stored? Enclosed storage spaces are great for hiding electrical equipment as well as keeping videos out of sight. Video players that are stored in an open area such as a TV stand should have the videos stacked on a shelf or bin nearby. While we're talking about videos, are they in labeled boxes so you know what is on each tape? Or will you pop in "George's Birthday Party" only to be greeted by a rerun of *Star Wars*? Preview and label the videos clearly, and group together the videos that can be reused to tape programs. Then, alphabetize your purchased videos for quick reference.

Are you constantly looking for the remote control or *TV Guide*? Use Velcro® to park the remote on a lamp base or the TV. Create a little arm cover with a pocket to hang over your chair arm and keep the *TV Guide* and remote in it. Whoever shuts off the TV is responsible for putting the remote in its assigned spot.

Use Velcro® to attach game controllers to the top of the game console, and

*F*amilies with camcorders often find that their tapes become scattered and disorganized. Why not round up all the homemade videos for a family evening? Pop a bowl of popcorn, and settle in to watch videos you've taped of the family over the years; then vote on the ones that stay and the ones that can be used for retaping.

label them so that you can easily identify what they go with. Keep the games in their cases near the TV on a shelf or in a cabinet. Keeping the game CDs, DVDs, and cartridges in a box or plastic container makes it easier to put everything away and find it again. Label the end of the container so that you know at a glance what's in it.

Magazines—Don't Subscribe to Clutter

Be open-minded about the types of storage you can use in your family and living room areas. For instance, wicker wastebaskets are great for storing magazines. When my son was younger and into hot-rod magazines, our magazines were always combined in one basket and while he searched for his, mine ended up on the floor. To solve the problem, I purchased several square wicker wastebaskets from the dime store (that would be the dollar store these days), and stacked the baskets on top of each other on their sides, snugly between the wall and the TV—they looked like cute little wicker cubbyholes! In one basket we kept his magazines and books, and in the other I separated my books and magazines and papers. Each of us was responsible for sorting out the baskets every month or so. He clipped articles he wanted to save from the magazine and stored them in a binder in his room. That solved a major clutter problem and kept our family room organized. Over the years, those baskets got used for lots of things, including towels in the guest bath (rolled up and tucked inside), craft supplies, and more. To this day, I still have a couple of baskets lurking in my storage closet to hold umbrellas, scarves, and earmuffs.

By the Book(case!)

Bookcases and wall units are great, but as so often happens, the unit is filled up on the day it is delivered, and five years later it's still holding the same books and now, outdated catalogs. Go through your books from time to time.

Unpack the bookcase shelf by shelf and look at each book. If you have already read it five times or didn't find it to your taste the first three times you tried to read it, then donate it to a senior center or some other worthy cause. If the kids are teenagers, perhaps it's time to either box up for sentimental reasons or pass on those preschool books. And what about that accounting textbook from the course you took four years ago? These books change annually, and frankly, that 1998 textbook isn't likely to be worth the paper it's printed on. Time to recycle.

Make sure you take a look at your CD collection too. Our taste in music changes. If you have CDs that you haven't listened to in years, give them a try. If they appeal to you, fine; if not, it's time to donate them or put them in the garage-sale collection. If the kids—who are now thirty with homes of their own—have a heavy metal collection taking up space, box it and give it back to them. And if you have a couple of boxes filled with cassettes, but no cassette player, now's the time to get rid of them too.

Putting It All Together

To get you started with your own unique storage needs, why not consider some of these ideas?

- Look around your own home first. Is there a seldom-used bookcase in one of the kids' rooms? Perhaps there's a nightstand collecting dust in the guest bedroom. Either one of these items is a great storage solution. The bookcase can be used as is, if the finish complements the family room furniture, or a quick coat of paint can transform it into a decor piece for storage. Work with the nightstand by adding a coat of paint, or even covering it with a few leftover scraps of wallpaper that match the room.

- Storage boxes from the discount store can be covered in paper to match your decor or in leftover wallpaper to match the room. These can be stored in view and still look nice. Sturdy boxes last the longest and work best, so before you toss out boxes from beverages or laundry detergent, take a second look at them.

- Store craft supplies such as crochet hooks, knitting yarn and needles, and needlepoint projects in an attractive basket near your favorite chair. Purchase a wicker basket in the right size at a discount store or

*W*hen selecting furniture for the family room, remember to look for hidden storage options. Hinged ottomans that open up for storage inside, tables with lots of drawers, and shelving that is open on top and has doors on the bottom to keep things out of sight but still handy, are all good options.

garage sale, and don't worry if the color doesn't match. Just zap it with a coat of spray paint (available in a dizzying array of colors for about $1 per can) to match your room. Even a briefcase can be used. It's easy to store and pick up and carry with you.

- Consider a sturdy plastic basket on wheels or with handles to hold kids' toys. This can be easily moved around the room and holds plenty of blocks, dolls, and toys. A square bin turned on its side is wonderful for storing board games too.

- Use empty oatmeal boxes to store Legos and other toys that come in small pieces. Again, cover the boxes in colored fabric, wallpaper, or adhesive backed paper to match your decor. These boxes are great because they're sturdy and come with a lid that is easy for kids to remove and put back. Don't overlook those potato chip canisters with plastic lids either.

- Wicker hampers are perfect for storing afghans and throws, for those chilly evenings, and also favorite "TV watching" pillows.

Of course, these great storage ideas aren't handy unless the family learns to use them. Every evening, just before leaving the room, each person should remove things that don't belong, such as slippers, socks, food dishes, homework, and school or craft projects. Once family members are in the habit of doing this, it will take only a few minutes to tidy up. Even the smallest child can help by picking up their things too. The important thing is to have handy storage so that the cleanup is not a project, but rather a quick act of tidying up.

Great Scott! It's the Great Room

If your home was built in the last fifteen years or so, you may face a new challenge: the great room. This room combines family living and formal living in one space. Needless to say, it also poses a unique motivation to stay organized, since it is a "family" and "guest" room in one. It can be difficult to combine the casualness of family living and the desire for a more formal, less lived-in and cluttered look. How you arrange the room and the storage options you use will determine your success and your happiness with this room.

The interesting thing about a great room is that the very openness that you love can create storage chaos. These rooms tend to attract clutter from other rooms such as the kitchen and the entry. Concealed storage and shelving storage is best for this room. Built-ins are ideal, but freestanding units with doors can also work well. If you have the space, consider turning one wall into a combination of bookcases and cabinets. It will look great, and the storage options are endless. You can find inexpensive bookcases at home centers or even at garage sales. Bring them home and finish with stain or paint

"My husband said he needed more space. So I locked him outside."

—*Roseanne*

to complement the room's decor. When buying used furniture, keep in mind the size and style you need. Sometimes what looks good sitting in the driveway can be all wrong once it is in your room. I always carry my room measurements with me when I shop. That way when I stumble on a great "find," I can measure to see if it will fit the room.

In the great room you definitely want to do away with what I call the doodad ditties. Make your decorating statement with larger pieces, and assign the small collections and knickknacks to another area of your home. If this is the room where you want to store your collectibles, consider a glass-fronted cabinet to keep things out of the way and eliminate weekly dusting and the chance of breakage.

If you are storing lots of small items in closed cupboards, consider these storage options:

- Small plastic boxes from the dollar store (or raid your daughter's cosmetics box) work well.
- Shoe boxes are another old favorite.
- TV dinner trays have handy little compartments (wash them out first, of course!).
- Fishing tackle boxes are ideal for teeny-tiny items.
- Styrofoam® egg cartons work well for miniature objects. Label the tops of the cartons with a marker and you won't even have to guess at the contents!
- Plastic ice cube trays are also great storage containers for small items.
- Tool boxes are great and come in a wide range of sizes.

- Remember, storage containers do not have to come from expensive stores. Think "recycle"—gift boxes, coffee cans, plastic bowls from the kitchen . . . you get the idea.

One last reminder: Even though you have wonderful cabinets with doors, don't use that as a license to fill up every inch of space and store items you haven't looked at or used in years. If you allow yourself to collect, and stuff your cabinets, you'll soon outgrow them.

Formally Yours—The Living Room

Are you fortunate enough to have a separate room apart from family living quarters that houses a piano, a well-loved book collection, or a crackling fireplace? Then you have what we used to call a formal living room. Today, these rooms are often taking on a new life as a music room or library, as well as a seating area.

Bear in mind that pianos should be placed near an inside wall for easier climate control. These delicate instruments are very sensitive to changes in temperature, even just overnight, and deviations in temperature can require more frequent tuning. Adequate humidity is also important for your piano; if the air in your home is dry, consider adding a humidifier. Your piano is an heirloom that can be passed down from generation to generation, so you'll want to take good care of it. Don't forget to add a hinged piano bench. They're handy for storage of sheet music and odds and ends too.

This is also a good room in which to house collections of beautiful objects. Whether you collect seashells or figurines, a display of them in a corner cabinet would complement the decor nicely. However, keep in mind that these items aren't called dust-catchers for nothing. Along with a weekly vacuuming, you'll need to dust in here once a week, so be sure the items you store here have meaning to you.

In this room your storage needs will be minimal, since it is more of a "sit and visit" room. Incorporate storage ideas from the family room and great room as you need them. Think in terms of closed cabinets and using drawer space in tables for such things as coasters and small napkins, anything that you might need when you entertain guests in this room.

Keeping it tidy and clutter-free means you, your family, and your guests get to enjoy the finer things in life comfortably.

CHAPTER 6

Kitchen Duty

*T*hings in your home may become scattered far and wide, but chances are your kitchen is like the mother ship in a Star Wars movie—everything eventually comes back here to roost! The kitchen is the hub of most family activities, and it's also the place where conquering clutter and becoming organized really pays off. Your kitchen can be a joy to use when things are easy to find and there is logic guiding the tasks you need to do. The proper use of your storage space is the factor that will determine how user-friendly your kitchen is.

Counter Attack

Since the countertop space is always at a premium in the kitchen—*location, location, location*—the idea here is to eliminate as much as possible. The rule of thumb for kitchen appliances is that if you don't use an item at least every other day, then it can be stored in a cupboard or pantry just as conveniently. So unplug your bread maker, espresso machine, or Crock-Pot™ and store it on the bottom shelf of your kitchen pantry, in the cupboard above your refrigerator, or in the back of the pots-and-pans cupboard.

Now, survey what remains and begin by grouping related items together.

- Keep the coffee, measuring spoons, and filters in a cupboard close by the coffeemaker. A small plastic basket with rubber suction cups that adhere to your fridge is great for storing coffee filters.

- If you have a bread box, put it and the toaster together, so that making toast is convenient.

- Group your canisters near the cupboard that contains your baking supplies.

- Keep your vegetable basket near the sink where you prepare the vegetables, and keep it out of the sun, so that your onions and potatoes don't spoil quickly.

- Keep your dish soap and other supplies in the cabinet under the sink, so that you don't take up precious counter space. Or, if you prefer, put the big container of dish soap under the sink, and keep a small liquid-soap hand pump filled with detergent next to the tap.

- Cutting boards can be hung on the wall.

- Use a magnetic strip to hold often-used tools such as bottle and can openers—or, in some houses, pizza cutters!

Take a good look around and do what you need to in order to have an uncluttered work surface. Remember: The less counter clutter you have to deal with, the less time you'll take to get the job done—whatever the job may be!

Inspector Gadget

Are you a "gadget-holic"? Then your counters are probably lined with intriguing but seldom-used items that were very appealing when demonstrated at the home show. Here you must be ruthless. Do you really use it? That wok you got in 1991 probably won't be useful if your Chinese cooking skills haven't advanced beyond heating up a package of frozen egg rolls. Ditto the fondue pot if you're lactose intolerant. Say good-bye and donate it or pass it on to a relative or friend. It now becomes their storage problem.

Away with Cupboard Clutter!

It's frustrating to open a cupboard and have a jumble of pots, pans, electrical cords, and lids spill out, isn't it? Let's conquer that cupboard clutter with a few simple steps. And for this task, let's use your *QUEEN*.

*Q*uestion: *What's not working in my cupboards? Do I have to sort through twenty spices to find the cinnamon? Does the flour always end up all over the shelf every time I take it out? Do I have pots, pans, pie plates, and cake pans all stored in a jumble? What do I need to* *do to make things in my cupboards more accessible, easier to take out and put away?*

*U*npack: I know it's tempting to shift things around in the cupboards and try to sort things out without unpacking, but that's like that old shell game—you're just moving things about that will soon show up elsewhere. So empty your cupboards first, one shelf at a time.

Once you've got everything out, fill a bucket with warm water and a squirt of your favorite dishwashing liquid or all-purpose cleaner, and give the insides of the cupboards a good cleaning. Rinse with clear water and wipe dry. Get rid of all that sticky stuff that attracts bugs.

This suggestion may sound like a throwback to many of you, but consider lining your shelves with paper. Not only does it look pretty—shelf paper comes in a lot of lovely colors and patterns—it makes cleaning even easier. If you've used vinyl wallpaper on your

*W*hen arranging your cupboards, sometimes it is a good idea to draw up a plan. Determine what you will store where on paper. Group by logic and common sense.

kitchen walls, you might like to try that. Stay away from paper that sticks to the shelves, though; it's hard to put down and even harder to remove. A better alternative is to use a small roll of no-wax vinyl flooring, which can easily be cut to fit with a utility knife.

*E*valuate: I bet you can guess the next step: Now that you've removed everything, group like objects together. If you haven't baked a pie in three years, you probably don't need a pie tin. Do you still use the blender, the bread machine, and the fancy waffle maker? If the answer is no, then put them in the discard pile.

If you're clearing the cupboards in your pantry, have a good look at the canned goods. If there's a can of pumpkin pie filling that has been there since the Pilgrims landed, best get rid of it. Ever bought something in a three for $2 special, only to find out after the first can was opened that you didn't like it? Then why not donate the other two cans to a food bank?

While canned foods have a long shelf life, it's best not to keep them for more than a year, as the color, flavor, texture, and nutritive value can deteriorate. Canned goods should be stored at a temperature of 70 degrees and no higher than 95 degrees. Don't store them next to or over the stove area.

Pay close attention to the condition of canned goods. Discard bulging cans, because the food inside may be spoiled. Similarly, avoid buying cans with dents on the side seams or around the top and bottom rim seams. If a can is leaky, throw it away. Toss out rusty cans just to be on the safe side. Rust can penetrate the can and ruin the food inside.

*E*liminate: This is sometimes the tough one. Look through your discard pile. Box and bag things up for donation (food banks can always use cooking equipment), garage sale, or trash. Remove the boxes and bags from the room to give yourself working space, and to get rid of temptation.

*N*eaten Up: If you have made a diagram of where you want to store things, pull it out and get started. If you're more of a free thinker (read: someone who doesn't like writing things down), then think the process through before putting things away.

Here are some guidelines to help you get started:

- Nest frying pans and skillets, putting the largest on the bottom.
- Arrange pot lids in a sturdy empty box, or consider installing plastic storage baskets on the inside of your cabinet doors. Even an appropriate size old nightstand drawer with the knobs removed works well.
- Store cookie sheets and baking pans on their sides and slide into cupboards. Use a heavy bookend

or a brick wrapped in fabric to keep them standing. This not only saves space, but provides easy access too.

- Muffin pans, pizza pans, and some pot lids also slide well into those wire racks you get at stationery stores—the ones you use to prop up files.
- It's fine to pile plates and bowls on each other, but don't mix sizes and types.
- Keep the dishes you use most often at the front of the cupboard and the others at back.
- Save the storefront real estate for everyday items such as pots, pans, colanders, and lids.
- Keep little-used appliances such as espresso machines, pasta makers, and the like toward the back of the cupboard.
- Cast-iron skillets should be stored with a piece of wax paper inside to protect the finish from moisture and rust.
- A rack installed on the inside of the cupboard under the sink is perfect for holding aluminum foil, plastic wrap, and other similar products. You can find these racks at discount stores and home centers. Take advantage of awkward cupboard or drawer space for keeping them too. This will free up valuable storage space.
- Use cupboards near the stove to hold pots, pans, spatulas, and cooking spoons. It doesn't make sense to cross the room to get a pan every time you want to fry an egg.

*H*ere's a tip that will eliminate storing the same items day after day: Why not set the table for the next meal as you unload the dishwasher? Kids can be taught this task early on, saving Mom a little extra time each day.

Double Your Drawer Duty

Cleaning out the drawers is an important first step. Remove everything from each drawer, evaluate it, and then discard the trash or find new uses for it. Got some bits of string? The birds will love it for nesting—just tuck it outside in a branch of a tree. What about those old abused birthday candles. Use them for your next pity party. If you have leftover cards, use the fronts for gift cards and toss the rest. Now wash out the drawer with some baking soda and water or some all-purpose cleaner. Rinse and dry and you are ready to neaten up. Here are some double-duty drawer *(phew!)* storage tips:

- Store knives near your cutting board and cooking utensils near the stove. To reduce clutter on the counters, opt for a divided storage container in the drawers. To keep knives sharp and safely out of the way, use a knife storage container that holds them like a sheath. Knives slide in to keep your fingers safe and the finish protected too.

- If drawer space is tight, use a block-type countertop knife holder instead and a decorative ceramic pitcher or urn to hold cooking utensils such as spatulas, whisks, and wooden spoons. A clay flower pot makes a nice utensil holder. If you don't like the natural clay color, you can paint it to match the kitchen. Keep in mind that the more you store on the counter, the more you have to clean.

- Purchase under-the-counter drawers and knife holders at kitchen supply stores. These are ideal for small kitchen areas, or for those who love to cook and need additional storage space for their cooking tools.

Shelf Savvy

What your kitchen lacks in counter space can almost always be compensated for with the careful use of shelving. Look around your kitchen and you're sure to find plenty of wall space that can be put to use.

- Consider installing a shelf above the kitchen counter for your cookbooks. This keeps them handy but frees up valuable counter space.

- Everyone has a collection of favorite recipes. Did you know that your local bookstore carries blank cookbooks with divided vinyl sheets that can be used to hold your treasured family favorites? Assembling a family cookbook is a terrific project for summertime, when kids are out of school. When your recipes are all grouped together in one place, there's no more guessing where you wrote down Grandma's favorite bread pudding.

• Think of using shelves and wall hangers to hold other things you use daily too. Small hooks can hold mugs, kitchen towels, pot holders, and utensils.

• Storing Tupperware® and other plastic storage containers can really be frustrating. Of course, you can purchase storage systems for them, but you can also be creative. I like to devote a small upper cupboard, perhaps the one over the stove, to plastic storage. I stack my containers, by size and type, inside each other. Don't get the stacks too high or they will be frustrating to reach for and use. Stack the lids by size, with the largest against the cupboard wall, and use a bookend or a clean brick wrapped in plastic or fabric to hold them up. For smaller containers, use a low rectangular storage container to hold them. You can lift the large container out, select what you need, and then replace it without all of the plastic tumbling out. Weed out the bowls that are old and sticky and ones you never use—after all, you only have so many leftovers. If you run out of bowls, check the back of the refrigerator to see what is lurking unnoticed in a plastic bowl from dinner two months ago!

• Don't forget to use the space around your kitchen window. You can hang shelves here and arrange dishes, mugs, or even plants for a decorative and useful display.

• Store canned goods in a cool, dry cupboard. Group like items together, and for real ease, alphabetize them so that you can find what you are looking for in a hurry.

- Stored boxed items on a separate shelf and try the alphabetizing here too. This will also make quick work of putting the groceries away. If you have open boxes on the shelf, consider storing the contents in clear plastic containers. Keep any cooking directions you may need and tuck into the container.

- Once cookies are open, store them in a cookie jar or clear container on the shelf. This prevents scattering crumbs everywhere, keeps the cookies fresher, and also eliminates temptation for bugs.

- Spices and other flavorings lose their oomph after about six months (and in less time than that if they're stored near or in excessive heat and humidity), so replace yours frequently.

- Consider a tiered platform to hold spices. (You can find them in kitchen stores and catalogs.) The tiered rack allows you to see spices at a glance, making it much easier to get at the cardamom, or whatever spice you seem to use only at holidays.

- Make your own tiered spice racks by affixing three small shelves about the width of your spice jars to the inside of your cupboard or against a wall. Set up your spice center near the stove and baking center.

- Alphabetizing your spices is smart. Starting with anise in the front and tarragon in the back, you'll save yourself the time and trouble of having to look at each jar.

- Use pegboards for instant storage. Hang near the stove for ladles, spoons, and colanders. I have a friend who painted her pegboard to match her decor, then traced on it the outline of each item so that she could easily replace them after use. You can also stencil your pegboard to match a country, contemporary, or even high-tech kitchen.

- Pan holders that hang from the ceiling have been used in professional kitchens for years. Consider these especially if you have a center island in your kitchen (the pot rack can be suspended over the island), if you have a plethora of cooking pans, or if storage space is tight. Look in kitchen stores or catalogs for these racks, or even make your own.

Shopping Smarts

Let's consider how you shop. Do you stop at the grocery store almost daily to purchase a few apples, a half pound of hamburger, and a jar of pickles? Or are you a "stocker," in love with warehouse stores?

Stockers will require more storage than most regular pantries can provide. Here you need to consider alternate storage, and don't hesitate to get creative. Although I wouldn't advocate it, a friend of mine who loved baking stored 50-pound bags of sugar behind her living room couch! Perhaps a hall closet in which you have installed extra shelves or a designated area in the basement where you've installed some shelving or a freestanding unit would hold your purchases. Keep a contents list posted in your "alternate pantry" so that you

*E*veryone has seen those three-tiered hanging fruit baskets. Why not use them to hold boxes of your favorite tea, or granola bars for the kids. These inexpensive space-makers are very handy.

don't continually stock up on the same items (an occupational hazard for professional shoppers). This also allows you to use up what's on the shelves. This extra pantry space is also a boon for those who enjoy canning their own fruits and vegetables.

Those of you lucky enough to have an extra freezer or refrigerator know how handy they can be to store things you won't need every day. Put a sheet of paper on the front listing what is inside and attach with a magnet. Cross off an item when you remove it and you'll always know what you have. This eliminates reaching into the freezer and finding that year-old package of hamburger with freezer burn.

Store meat in the freezer in freezer wrap. Look for this in your grocery store on the aisle with plastic wrap and aluminum foil. This protects meat from freezer burn for up to a year. Make sure you label the outside of the wrap with the contents of the package and date of purchase. A permanent marker or grease pencil works well for this. Remember to store your food in the freezer according to date, with the freshest food in the back.

Let me share something I learned the hard way. Plug a

nightlight that you can easily see into the same plug as the freezer or refrigerator. Use a red Christmas bulb to make it really stand out. In case of a power outage, you will quickly see that the light is out and you'll be able to take steps more quickly to protect your food investment. Not only does this help keep food from spoiling and save you a nasty cleanup job; it can actually save your appliance from dying a nasty death due to an odor that can't be removed.

Pack a Pretty Pantry

Consider turning several cupboards into a pantry if there is not a designated one in your home. Installing a freestanding cupboard in or near the kitchen works too. Think sliding shelves here for maximum storage. There are firms who can turn stationary shelves into ones that slide; they charge a flat rate per shelf. Ask friends for a recommendation or look under "Shelving" in the Yellow Pages.

- Make maximum use of your pantry by grouping items together as you use them. Store rice, pasta, and packaged potatoes together, and canned tomato sauce, mushrooms, and vegetables nearby. At mealtime, you can see at a glance what's available to be prepared.

- Store spice packages such as taco seasoning in an empty berry basket for easy reference.

- Store open containers of flour, sugar, rice, and cereal in clear square containers. Square containers work

better than round in terms of the amount of space they take up. Plastic is better than glass, which can break. Buy containers that will stack on top of each other and you'll save even more room.

• Another alternative to containers is to use sturdy resealable plastic bags. I like to make my own colored sugar for baking cookies, for example. I just mix a few drops of food coloring with white sugar and store each color in plastic bags. These are much less expensive than containers of "decorative sugar" and this is a fun project kids always like to help with too.

*S*toring dry foods such as cereal, brown sugar, and flour in plastic containers eliminates the problem of bugs in open packages.

• Leave the lowest or most inconvenient shelf for items like Jell-O mix, cooking oil, extra ketchup, syrup, and other condiments you reach for only occasionally.

• Double-tiered plastic lazy Susan racks are available at most discount stores. Consider this option if you have limited storage space, as each of these racks can hold plenty of canned goods and are easily accessed.

• Arrange taller cans in back and shorter items in front.

- Place the goodies everyone forages for right up front, where they are readily available, so that no one has to dig through the entire pantry for the Ding Dongs®. You'll keep order that way.

- Consider labeling shelves by applying a piece of masking tape and writing with a marker where each item goes. One row for canned soups, another for fruits, one for cereals, and so on. For families with children, this not only makes putting away groceries a breeze, it gives the kids a reading lesson every time!

*W*hen we were children, our basement pantry always held an extra supply of canned soup, with the shelves labeled by color. Yellow was chicken noodle, red was tomato, and blue was bean with bacon. At lunchtime, we were instructed to go to the basement and bring up "two cans of red and one can of blue soup." It worked!

The "Junque" Drawer

Repeat after me: "I give myself permission to have a junk drawer." Yes, even the Queen has one! Mine has a couple of screwdrivers, some pliers, pens, paper, a couple of puzzling screws (if I ever figure out where they go, the puzzle will be solved), a flashlight, some thumbtacks, and even a few new cat-nip balls, in case the cat ever has a toy emergency. When the drawer gets too jumbled (about every other month), I just haul the wastebasket over to it and remove everything, put things away in their proper places, and then I'm ready to start again. Allowing yourself one junk drawer means you won't get in the habit of using any convenient space to stuff things in.

The Fridge

The refrigerator and freezer take a lot of abuse. There isn't a person alive, I venture, who hasn't peered into the depths of their refrigerator at one time or another and pulled out a "mystery bowl" lurking somewhere in the back. To stop the science experiments, use these tried-and-true methods.

Clean out the refrigerator and freezer separately, starting with the refrigerator. First remove the entire contents of the refrigerator, examining things as you go to determine what is a keeper and what can be disposed of. Have a sturdy trash bag standing by to receive any "mystery items." Use a cooler to keep perishables cold while you work. (Don't worry, this won't take long!) "Keepers" are condiments such as ketchup, mustard, and salad dressings—if they are still fresh.

A quick word of advice: Even condiments have an expiration date. They last, open in your refrigerator, for about 12 to 18 months. Take a look at them as you replace them in the refrigerator. If they have changed color or look excessively watery, it's time to toss and restock. And remember, when you are using perishable items such as mayonnaise or salad dressing, return them to the refrigerator as soon as possible to keep them fresh longer.

Now's the time to thoroughly clean the interior of the refrigerator. Remove glass shelves or racks one by one to clean them. As you take them out, wash the wall areas of the refrigerator that can be reached. A mild solution of 1 gallon of warm water and a couple of squirts of dishwashing liquid and 1–2 tablespoons of borax will do the job nicely. Mix this up in the sink or a bucket, and use a sponge or soft cloth. You probably found that box of baking soda in the back that has been deodorizing the refrigerator for months. Remove it and sprinkle some of the baking soda on a damp cloth to remove stubborn food spills from the walls and shelves. When you're done, you can place the box with your cleaning supplies, for many other uses around the house. Put a fresh box in the refrigerator. Wash and rinse the shelves and dry with a soft cloth; then replace them in the refrigerator. Here you'll want to put a coat of Clean Shield® on the shelves before putting items back. This wonderful product creates a nonstick finish that is stain- and soil-resistant. You can mop up spills in your refrigerator with just a damp sponge, making cleanup a lot easier.

- Group keepers by type. Store salad dressings, horseradish, and other condiments together in the door. Jams and jellies can stay here too. Check the dates on your perishables and dispose of anything that's past its prime. Consider how you use things in the refrigerator. If the kids are constantly reaching into the back for the jelly, for instance, move it up front and store less frequently used items in the back.

- Dairy products such as cottage cheese, yogurt, and sour cream should be stored in their original containers. Hard cheese will stay freshest if stored wrapped in foil, wax paper, or plastic wrap after opening.

- Group fruits and vegetables separately, each in their own crisper bins. This way you can pull open the drawer and know if you need to pick up a head of lettuce or some more apples. This also keeps your produce fresher longer, as fruits and vegetables emit gases that cause each other to deteriorate; grouping like things together will keep these vapors from mingling. Remember not to wash produce prior to storage, as this speeds up deterioration.

*I*s your refrigerator the place where you keep the leftovers until it's time to throw them out?

- A separate section of the refrigerator just for leftovers is a good idea. This keeps you from overlooking them. Store them in see-through containers, and hopefully you won't shove them to the back to linger for six months! Remove any leftovers from cans and store in plastic or glass to keep a metallic taste from ruining the food. Leftovers need to be refrigerated no more than two hours after cooking, so be sure to store them as soon as mealtime is over. As you store your leftovers in the refrigerator, make a list of them and tack it to the refrigerator door. You'll be more apt to remember and to use them and you'll never find a mystery bowl next time you clean.

• Perishables such as eggs should be stored on the top shelf of the refrigerator. Remember that the door is often the warmest place in your refrigerator, and that's where the egg container usually is. It's much safer to store your eggs in their original container until they're used. For this reason, you'll want to store your butter, margarine, and cream cheese on the top shelf too. Leave the door area for your sturdier condiments, such as ketchup and mustard.

• Store meats on the bottom shelf if your refrigerator doesn't have a meat tray. This prevents them from dripping on other items, in case the wrapping isn't tight. Thaw a roast or other large cut of meat inside a bowl, so that as it defrosts the juice will run into the bowl, not all over your shelves.

• If your family drinks a lot of canned juices and soft drinks, a can rack will come in handy. Here's where an extra refrigerator is a bonus too, to hold beverages you buy on sale or use frequently. A word of warning: Do not place warm cans of soda in the freezer to quickly cool them off. The carbonation causes the can to burst. Not a pretty sight.

*D*on't overcrowd the refrigerator, as the premise for keeping food cool is that interior air is allowed to circulate. You'll want to set the temperature dial to less than 40 degrees to keep harmful bacteria from growing. Look for a refrigerator thermometer at home stores; leaving one in your refrigerator will help you keep your food fresher longer.

Leftovers? Think Again!

By now you probably have collected partially used bottles and containers with just a little left in them. Here's what you can do with those leftovers.

- That old odor-absorbing box of baking soda—put it down the kitchen drain followed by ½ to 1 cup of white vinegar for a fresh-smelling, clear-flowing drain.
- Lemon juice—clean your brass with lemon juice by adding salt. Rub it on, rinse, and dry well. Clean stains off counters with a paste of lemon juice and cream of tartar. Remove rust from hard surfaces or white fabrics by putting the lemon juice on the rust. For fabric, lay it out in the sun.
- Ketchup—now's the time to shine that copper by rubbing it with ketchup until it shines. Rinse and dry well.

lear soda water that's lost its fizz—use to wipe down white appliances for a great shine. Buff with a soft cloth. Clear soda water also adds vigor to plants and cut flowers.

- If that onion is not good enough for the salad, remove rust from your utensils, such as paring knives, by sticking them in the onion and letting them sit until the rust is removed, usually a matter of hours.

- Put citrus peels from citrus fruit past its prime down the garbage disposal to freshen and deodorize.

- If that potato isn't looking great, cut it in half and rub it on white shoes. Let the shoe dry, and then polish for a streak-proof shine. Or, remove mud from clothes by rubbing with the cut side of a potato.

- Add shine to a wood table by polishing with that last bit of mayonnaise in the jar. Rub it in well and buff with a soft cloth.

Store It Safely

Here is a list of the most commonly stored foods. You may be surprised as you look over the list at the storage life of some foods. The manual that comes with your refrigerator and the web site *www.fightbac.org* can provide you with additional information.

Bacon (cooked)
1 week

Bacon (uncooked)
2 weeks

Bread Dough
3 to 4 days

Butter
1 to 3 months

Cheese (hard)
6 months

Cheese (soft, opened)
1 to 2 weeks

Cheese (soft, unopened)
3 to 4 weeks

Chicken (fresh)
1 to 2 days

Eggs (hard-boiled)
1 week

Eggs (fresh in shell)
3 to 5 weeks

Fish (fresh)
1 to 2 days

Fish (cooked)
3 to 4 days

Fruit or Pumpkin Pies (baked)
2 to 3 days

Fruit or Pumpkin Pies (unbaked)
1 to 2 days

Gravy or Meat Broth
1 to 2 days

Mashed Potatoes
3 to 4 days

Meat (cooked)
3 to 4 days

Olives and Pickles
1 month

Poultry (cooked)
3 to 4 days

Soups and Stews
2 to 4 days

Steaks, Roasts, Chops (uncooked)
3 to 5 days

Stuffing (cooked)
3 to 4 days

Turkey (fresh)
1 to 2 days

White Wine (recorked)
1 to 2 days

Here are some other things that you may want to store in the refrigerator:

- Nail polish (lasts much longer)
- Medicines that require cooler temperatures (check labels)
- Face gels and eye masks
- Facial toner for a cool mist on a hot day
- Exposed film

Now that you have the refrigerator organized, keep food-stuffs in the same area, so that when you unpack groceries after a trip to the store, you will store things in the proper place without thinking. Before you shop for food, make sure you look over the refrigerator and wipe up any spills; use warm water with a little baking soda and white vinegar added. Throw out what is past its prime, and you're ready to restock.

Here's a helpful tip: If you have a computer, make up a master list of foods you commonly buy, such as milk, cheese, eggs, lunch meat, apples, ice cream, and so on. I like to set mine up in the order I shop—produce first, then meats, canned goods, and frozen foods. Make up copies of the list, and keep a copy posted on your refrigerator with a magnet. Add a checkmark as each item is depleted. That way you can know just what to shop for; you can also add other items to the bottom of the list as you need them. (If you'd like a head start, just visit my Web site *www.queenofclean.com* and download my grocery list!)

The Deep Freeze

Now it's time to venture into the depths of the freezer. Remove the food from your freezer, check the freshness date, and throw out anything that is no longer good. Place the things you will be putting back in a cooler to keep them cold.

- Wipe out the freezer with warm water and a little white vinegar before restocking. Make sure your meat is labeled and wrapped in freezer paper to prevent freezer burn. Sometimes standing meat on its edge instead of stacking makes it easier to see what you have and takes up less room. Keep all meat together.

- Now group frozen vegetables. You might consider an expandable freezer shelf to double your space; these shelves are available at home stores and kitchen centers. Place it over the first layer of food and stack bags and boxes of vegetables, frozen egg rolls, waffles, or frozen side dishes, over it. Remember to keep desserts separate from the rest of the food, so that they aren't crushed or lost in the shuffle. Try to store the packages so that you can see part of the printed label; they will be easier to identify.

- When bringing food home, place the newest food in the back of the freezer and move older products to the front, to be used first.

- Keep a plastic container in the freezer door to hold ice if your unit does not have an automatic icemaker. You can easily empty ice trays all at once into the container and then refill the trays so that you always have enough ice on hand.

Don't Get Burned—Freezer Burned, That Is...

Keep this handy frozen food storage chart in mind when filling your freezer.

Egg (raw yolks and whites)
1 year

Egg Substitute (unopened)
1 year

Butter/Margarine
(do not freeze whipped butter)
6 to 9 months

Cheese (hard)
6 weeks

Ice Cream, Sherbet (cover top with plastic wrap)
2 months

Milk
1 month

Fruits (berries, peaches, pears, etc.)
12 months

Frozen Juices
6 months

Frozen Vegetables
8 months

TV Dinners, Frozen Casseroles
3 to 4 months

Prestuffed Chicken Breasts or Pork
Don't freeze well

Raw Hamburger and Stew Meats
3 to 4 months

Ground Turkey, Veal, Pork or Lamb (or mixture)
3 to 4 months

Lean Fish (cod, haddock, sole, flounder)
6 months

Fatty Fish (perch, mackerel, salmon)
2 to 3 months

Lobster Tails
3 months

Shrimp (uncooked)
12 months

Oysters
4 months

Scallops
3 months

Ham (canned, unopened)
Don't freeze

Ham (canned, opened)
1 to 2 months

Ham (fully cooked)
1 to 2 months

Ham Slices (fully cooked)
1 to 2 months

Hot Dogs and Lunch Meats
1 to 2 months

Soups and Stews
2 to 3 months

Bacon
1 month

Sausage (raw)
1 to 2 months

Smoked Breakfast Links and Patties
1 to 2 months

Steaks
6 to 12 months

Chops
4 to 6 months

Roasts
4 to 12 months

Cooked Meat and Meat Dishes
2 to 3 months

Gravy and Meat Broth
2 to 3 months

Fresh Chicken and Turkey (whole)
1 year

Fresh Chicken and Turkey (parts)
9 months

Fried Chicken
4 months

Chicken Nuggets and Patties
1 to 3 months

As you can see, the length of time that foods can safely be frozen varies greatly. When you stock up on an item, keep in mind how long you can store it frozen before it's eaten. Purchasing items on sale, then having to dispose of them uneaten is what's known as a "false economy."

Congratulations on completing a job you've probably been putting off since you moved into your house. Now that your kitchen is reorganized and tidy, reward yourself. How? With dinner at your favorite restaurant, of course!

CHAPTER 7

The Paper Chase

It seems that the farther we advance with technology, the more we are inundated with paper. Remember when computer gurus told us we would soon be living in a paperless society? Well, guess what—it seems that the technical revolution has generated a whole new spawn of paperwork.

The vast majority of waste in recycling sites is nothing more than ordinary paper—everything from junk mail, newspapers, magazines, and phone books to the flotsam-and-jetsam paperwork of everyday life. Controlling this particular area of clutter is key to living a less stressful and simpler life. Let's tackle the paper chase together, shall we?

You've Got Mail

When you pick up your mail every day, bring it in the house to the same spot. It can be a basket in the entryway, a designated spot on the kitchen counter, or a space at your desk in the home office. Then take a few moments to go through your mail, and remember the rule to handle each piece of paper only once. Newspapers, catalogs, and magazines go to the magazine rack or a basket, where you can find them and read them at your leisure. Toss out the old catalog as you replace it with the new issue, and make sure to sort through this storage bin regularly (weekly is great) to keep it up-to-date. Toss the water, electric, or car payment into a manila folder or large envelope marked "Bills" for payment. Read personal mail, such as wedding or shower invitations, birthday cards, and the like, and enter information on your family calendar. Scan through junk mail, then toss. The big temptation here is to set down a letter, bill, or "interesting idea" from the junk mail for "later." However, later usually doesn't come! Teach yourself to clear out your mail daily, and clutter has that much less of a chance to congregate.

Consider how many charge accounts you have. Do you really need four major credit cards, a gasoline card, and a card for every department store in your nearby mall? Remember that all of these cards generate reams of mail in your direction from these retailers. Simplify your life by cutting down your credit cards to just a few you can use everywhere.

Chances are you're on some mailing lists for items that no longer interest you. Take 15 minutes today to stop the accumulation of unwanted offers in the mail. You'll need to make one phone call and write a single letter to do this. To stop unwanted credit offers, dial 1–888–5–OPT–OUT at any time of day or night. Then, write to the following: DMA Mail Preference Service, PO Box 643, Carmel, NY 10512. Include your complete name, address, zip code, and a request to "activate the preference service." The Direct Marketing Association estimates that this one step will stop 75 percent of junk mail from reaching you for up to five years. Keep in mind this option may stop catalogs and promotions you would have liked to receive.

The Paper Tiger

And some ways to tame it:

- Think twice before you copy that e-mail or print that delicious recipe you want to try "someday." The great temptation of the Internet is that it makes so much information available so easily. How may times have you printed out a couple of pages to read later, and later has never come? And how many times have you printed out one page only to be flooded with six or seven? Remember: You don't have to print everything. The information will be there, on line, the next time you need it.

- Reuse paper in your printer to copy items for personal use; save the clean copy paper for items you need to send out or keep as a personal record.

- Consider using electronic or on-line banking—it cuts down dramatically on paperwork.

- Recycle or toss newspapers and magazines at least weekly. Piles of old newspapers are untidy, and a fire hazard as well.

- Store important personal papers such as your will, birth certificate, social security card, and passport in a safe place at home (a fireproof box is best) or a safe deposit box at the bank. If you store these papers at the bank, keep a list of what is in the safe deposit box on your computer or in your home files. Go through these papers twice a year to make sure they're in order. Keep a separate folder for each child in your family. In each, place their immunization record, report cards, birth certificates, social security card, and any other important information, such as allergies, doctors' names and phone numbers. This will be invaluable, especially at the beginning of each school year.

- A family calendar is a great idea. Purchase a large one and post it in an obvious place such as the kitchen. Mark down birthday parties, weddings, family parties, as invitations arrive. Keep a clothespin attached to the calendar, where you can hang the invitation or pertinent information. When the event is over, just toss.

When you control the flow of paperwork in your home, you'll feel more in control of your life, and your time is then spent the way you prefer. That means more quality time for you and your family, as well as more time for the fun things in life.

> "I read about eight newspapers
> a day; when I'm in a town with only one
> newspaper, I read it eight times."
>
> —Will Rogers

CHAPTER 8

Memories

*A*re you the one with the family photos still in their store envelopes complete with the receipt still stapled to the flap? Is your spoon collection tossed into the bottom drawer of the china cabinet? Are your miniature race cars going nowhere fast in that old broken-down box in the basement? Collections can be wonderful, but if they are stored away carelessly—or not stored at all—your precious treasures can become clutter. And who wants to inherit clutter?

Collections can also breed out of control and take over your living space. If you are allotting more space to your collections than to where you eat and sleep, it's time to pick out the few collections that mean the most to you and part with the rest.

Researchers say that most folks collect for five basic reasons:

- *Love of beauty.* There's just something soothing about contemplating a snowy white teacup with a pristine rose etched on the front.

- *A sense of satisfaction in completion.* Ask any ten-year-old boy how he feels when he rounds out his baseball card collection.

- *The thrill of the chase.* This appeals to the hunter-gatherer in all of us. Plus, it adds a little pizzazz to shopping trips, vacations, and forays to yard sales when we have a specific item in mind.

- *To go back to our roots.* Many collectibles are rich in cultural and ethnic meaning.

- *Profit.* This is usually the last reason most people acquire collections, but of course artwork, coins, and other high-end items can become quite valuable.

Almost everyone has a collection. Let's look at how to manage one without letting it turn into clutter or take over your house.

Photo Opportunity

While there are as many types of collections as there are collectors, it's a pretty safe bet that most of us have an unwieldy photo collection, so we'll start with that. Round up all of your photographs. Yes, even the ones in the junk drawer and your underwear drawer. Sit down with a trash bag nearby and sort the good from the bad and the just plain ugly . . . no, I don't mean Uncle Fred doing his weird toupee trick! Look at each photo closely. If any of them are out of focus, have red eyes, look like something from *MAD* magazine, or are missing important parts (such as heads), throw them out NOW!

If you have good quality duplicate prints, pass them on to an interested relative or friend, otherwise toss those too.

Divide photos of children into a separate pile for each child. Organize the photos, starting with the most current, and label with names, dates, and any other pertinent information on the back. Next, organize the remaining photos, starting with the most current, and label with names, dates, locations, and any other information on the back. Start with the newest photos, so that by the time you reach oldies but goodies, you'll be more selective about what to keep and what to toss. Do you really need thirty-five pictures from David's birthday? Pick out the very best ones, and pass on or toss the others. Then label the outside of envelopes containing negatives with the date and location where the photos were taken.

Now it's time to consider how you want to store your photos. You can have a photo album per child, year, or event that the children can help with, or perhaps a photo box better suits your needs. You might want to consider grouping the photos by date, or event. If you recently built a home and have all the photos as the project went along, put those in an album beginning with the lot purchase and go through to completion. Add some personal thoughts too. You'll always cherish this memory, and the kids will love looking at it. To store pictures in a photo box, wrap them in acid-free tissue or select acid-free boxes to protect your photos over time. You can find these at craft and scrapbooking stores. If you prefer albums, be sure to choose those with plastic sleeves, rather than the sticky backs to preserve the quality of your photos. If you like scrapbooks best, be sure to pick one with acid-free paper to ensure a long life for your book.

Once you have your photo albums, scrapbooks, or boxes completed, make sure you label them on the outside and store them someplace accessible, such as the bottom shelf of your bookcase. The photos are now neatly organized and out of the way, but you can enjoy them and add to them at any time. Each time you bring home new photos, review them with a critical eye and toss any bad ones. Put the others in the albums, scrapbooks, or boxes as soon as possible.

You may wish to select some of your favorite photos to arrange in a collage-type frame (frames with multiple openings). These work especially well with a theme, such as family groups, vacations, holidays, or picnics—you get the idea. When your local discount store or art supply store has a sale on collage frames, stock up on half a dozen in a size you know you can use, and arrange these together as a display. Using identical frames will unify your collections and make them stand out. Of course, you can also get creative with frames and even make your own using those you've found at thrift shops, yard sales, or even in the attic. Small beads, seashells, ribbon, or charms add whimsy and flair to your frames and personalize your photo collection.

Let's Play Post Office

You've raided the mailbox, rummaged in the wastebaskets in the post office lobby and the office, and pestered your friends to save their envelopes. Now that you have all these wonderful stamps, what should you do with them? True, an ordinary shoe box gives storage space, but you should want a nicer place to store your collection—a place to display your material, not just store it. And, on the practical side, stamps and covers (envelopes with stamps on them, used in the mail) kept in a shoe box or paper folder risk damage from dirt or creases, losing value as well as beauty.

Purchasing your first album may be a kind of experiment. If you are buying an album in person, rather than by mail, listen to the seller's advice. Good beginners' albums are available that are not too expensive, are fully illustrated to show which stamp goes where, and may even contain extra information, such as maps and facts about the countries. Buy as wisely as you can and not over your budget, and don't be too discouraged if your first album turns out to be less than perfect. You will always need places for temporary storage as you continue in the hobby. Old albums never go to waste!

With experience you will soon learn what type of storage is best for you. Using care with these collections is important

*C*ollections such as stamps or coins, which can be stored in shoe boxes or sturdy metal containers, should be reviewed every six months or so (hey, you might have something valuable in there to trade on eBay™!). Stamp and coin albums should be dusted and kept along with any relevant books and supplies, such as magnifying glasses, nearby. Avoid storing them in damp basements or hot attics. A hall closet, bedroom closet, or even an empty drawer works well.

because you can pass them on to your children or grandchildren someday, along with some sage advice from you.

Letting the Cat out of the Bag

Lots of people collect representations of animals, pigs, cows, cats, dogs . . . you name it. For these collections, you can add a shelf down about 12 inches or so from the ceiling and let the animals march around the room. For expensive collections, enclosed storage is safer.

With Six You Get Egg Roll

There are always people who collect odd things. I had a friend who loved Chinese food and collected chopsticks from restaurants all over the country. To display them, he fashioned a fortune cookie out of foam and painted it to look like a cookie, complete with a fortune tag sticking out the side. He stuck his chopstick collection into the "cookie"! What I am saying is, be imaginative . . . think out of the box, or cookie, as the case may be.

Breaking Up Is Hard to Do

Do you collect breakables such as china or porcelain? China collections such as teacups or figurines do well attractively grouped in a glass-fronted hutch, but if you don't have one of these, use your imagination instead. Clear a space on a bookshelf or cabinet, arrange a pretty piece of fabric or doily, and display your treasures on that. Keep in mind that if you have little ones around, you will want to store your breakables up high where tiny hands can't reach.

For valuable collections of porcelain and other art objects, store them in locked, glass-fronted cabinets, or if the value is especially high, you may want to put these in a safe deposit box at the bank or in a safe. Keeping them secure should be your primary concern. Documenting their existence and value is your next step. Start by making a complete list of the pieces and add pertinent information, such as date of purchase, cost, information about the artist or creator of the piece, and any other relevant information. Take a photo of the object and attach the information to it and store in a safe place.

Other Collectibles

If someone in your family collects miniature race cars or Matchbox® vehicles, think of unique ways to display them. Perhaps roaring across the shelf of a bookcase, on the lower shelf of a table, or on shelving in your family room or den created to hold these treasurers. You can even mount them on wood strips and have them racing up the walls of the collector's bedroom. It's a good idea to list the place of purchase, date, and cost of each vehicle for your records and for resale purposes; keeping the box it came in can add value.

Anyone who collects spoons from every place he or she visits knows there is a vast variety of spoon racks available. Keep in mind that open racks will allow soiling and tarnishing of the spoons and require more upkeep. Glass-fronted spoon cabinets will keep the spoons clean and reduce the upkeep considerably. Spoon collections can add a lovely decorative touch to kitchens and dining rooms. Each time you bring home a spoon, you might want to consider labeling it with the date of purchase before you place it in the rack. Use a small sticky label for this purpose, and write with a permanent felt-tipped pen to preserve the information.

It Can Happen...

One last collective thought... before you throw out Aunt Gertrude's pottery collection, make sure that it is not a collector's item and of great value. There are many books in the library and web sites that can help you determine this. I had a friend who got the surprise of her life watching an antique show on TV. They showed a porcelain piece just like the one she was thinking of donating to a rummage sale that was valued at $3,200! Now, that's the extreme, but still keep it in mind.

CHAPTER 9

Putting on the Ritz

More than any other room in the house, the dining room is most often the setting for our happiest occasions, such as family dinners and birthday and holiday celebrations. What fun it is to envision a festive table spread with pretty dishes and a delicious feast, ready for our families and guests to enjoy. It can be more than a wonderful fantasy. With the right amount of organization, it can become a reality in your home.

The China Cabinet

Let's start with the china cabinet or sideboard. Remove everything, put sets of dishes in one group, crystal and stemware in another, and serving pieces such as large bowls and ladles in a third. Grouping like items together will help you find these things quickly when you need them.

The first thing I found when I started to declutter my dining room was that a lot of space was taken up with occasional

80

dishes. You know, the Christmas dishes you use once or twice and then store again, and the serving pieces that are only used on special occasions. Take a look in your china cabinet and sideboard and you'll know what I mean. These pieces take up valuable space that you could use to store things that you use frequently and make them easier to take out and put away. And the easier things are to use in your dining room, the more you'll want to use it, whether it's for an intimate family dinner or a gathering of the whole crowd.

As you are sorting things, think about what you want to keep and what you want to discard. If you haven't used them in years, consider selling them or passing them on to other family members. Just make sure you know their value before you decide to donate them to the thrift store. Many a person has given away a valuable antique! Don't let that happen to you. It's a good idea to take your older dishes and flatware to an antique dealer first, or even check out an on-line auction site like eBay. Many older china patterns are now collectibles.

Before putting items back in the cabinet, take the time to give it a good clean. Cabinets made of wood can be washed down with ordinary tea. Brew a strong pot of tea, using 2 or 3 tea bags, and let them steep for 15 minutes or so. Cool to room temperature, and wring out a soft cloth in

*R*epair or despair—it's up to you. If you're really going to glue the handle onto that china cup, do it now. Otherwise, out it goes . . .

the tea until damp. Then wipe the shelves and buff dry with a soft, clean cloth. The tannic acid in the tea adds luster to the wood finish. For plastic or metal buffets, sprinkle about a tablespoon of baking soda onto a soft cloth and wipe down the piece. Use a clean, damp cloth to rinse; then buff with a dry cloth. For glass shelves, a solution of equal parts rubbing alcohol and water will clean and create a shine.

When you start to rearrange things, put the seldom-used pieces, such as the Thanksgiving turkey platter, Christmas candlesticks, and eggnog cups, either up high or down low in areas that are harder to reach. (You're getting the hang of this, right?) Think about how you set your table as you put things away, and group the dishes and glasses that you use together near each other. You might consider wrapping groups of dishes in plastic or plastic wrap to keep them clean. You can also purchase zippered containers that fit dishes of various sizes to store your dishes in. Look for these containers at linen stores, organizing stores, or in specialty catalogs.

For more storage space, consider using a space-saving corner cabinet or some attractive cupboards or armoires. All of these cabinets can be adapted to your needs and will enhance your room style if chosen wisely. Built-ins, of course, are a wonderful option, especially those that are floor-to-ceiling with doors and perhaps a serving top.

Before purchasing new cabinets, make sure you measure your plates, trays, and other larger pieces, so that you don't get home with a new cabinet and find that you can't close the door because the plates stick out. Measuring will also ensure that you take full advantage of every bit of shelf space in your new cabinets. For small rooms, remember that glass shelves and glass-fronted units are not only attractive, but open up the area to the eye and are easy to clean.

Sturdy pieces with doors will work well for your dining room storage. Handles on doors will also help keep the front of the cabinet clean and unmarred. Look for hanging racks for cups and stacking units for dishes and things that will allow you to take advantage of the space within the cabinet. Store things where they are easily reached by you or the kids, whoever sets the table. Make it convenient to have help.

In a small dining room, don't overlook the storage use of areas around windows and doors. These small ledges will handle glasses and other knickknacks quite easily. Areas kept available for a bar service can be cleared and used for serving pieces. Use a portable bar cart to be set up when you are ready to serve cocktails.

Linens & Things & Napkin Rings

- To store table linens from the dining room, consider hanging tablecloths and their napkins on a padded hanger or on a plain wire hanger with an empty paper towel tube slipped over the bottom bar. Storing linens this way will keep creases to a minimum and make it easy for you to select exactly what you're looking for.

- Napkin rings can be placed in a plastic bag and hung over the neck of the hanger that's holding the tablecloth.

- Hang your linens in the back of the guest closet or any other closet where you have the room.

- Storing table linens in the basement is not a good idea. Moisture and humidity can cause mold and mildew that will ruin your fine cloths.

- Linens may be stored in the attic, but be sure to store them hanging and covered with a fabric cover, such as an old sheet. Don't use plastic, which can discolor the linens over time.

Heigh-Ho, Silver

- Sterling silver or silver-plated pieces will need to be wrapped in a silver-storage cloth to slow tarnishing. Line a drawer with this cloth and slide the silver in.

- Consider divided storage trays to store silverware and keep it organized. These trays are available in an array of styles. Measure your cabinet and select accordingly.

- Large silver pieces can be wrapped directly in storage cloths, or try silver storage bags that are specially treated to retard tarnish. Look for these cloths and bags in kitchen stores, linen stores, and specialty catalogs.

- Never use rubber bands or wrap silver in plastic wrap. These will accelerate tarnishing.

Now that your dining room is clutter-free, you are ready to fulfill your fantasy of hosting a feast fit for a King—or maybe a Queen!

CHAPTER 10

The Throne Room

*N*o matter what size your bathroom is, you'll never have enough storage. Since it's also the room we most hate to clean (I've taken an informal royal survey!), it presents us with some unique challenges in conquering clutter. But start with this premise, *Less clutter means less cleaning,* and you can't go wrong.

Before you tackle this project, consider the traffic. Who uses the room—just one person, several family members, or is it a guest bath used only infrequently? Any time more than one person uses a bathroom, it's a good idea to assign each individual his or her own area for storage. This can be as simple as assigning a shelf or a portion of a shelf, grouping containers together for grooming aids, or declaring one half of the counter "his" and one half "hers." But before you start on this, let's add another person to the mix—let's bring along your *QUEEN*, and work through this clutter-clearing program step-by-step-by-step.

*Q***uestion:** *Look around. What things in the bathroom are really working? What things do I like—what things do I hate? Am I wasting time every morning digging for essentials? Is my blow dryer tangled in its cord? How many times have I been late leaving the house because I had to search for my curling iron or razor among all of the clutter that has accumulated?*

*U***npack:** You'll be familiar with this step by now. Working with one area at a time, take everything out of the medicine cabinet, remove the bottles from the side of the bath, and unpack the cabinet under the sink. Remove towels from the cupboards and toiletries from the vanity. Once you have everything emptied out, you can look it all over and decide what to keep. Be sure to work with just one area at a time, though. Otherwise you'll have an unholy mess!

*E***valuate:** Think your bathroom is home to just soap and towels? Think again!

- Start with the larger things, such as towels and washcloths. Look them over to determine if any of them should become rags.

- Weed out the hot rollers you used in the '80s, your husband's sideburn trimmer that he used when he had sideburns . . . and hair, and all of those headband and hair ornaments you used when you had long hair.

- Try your blow dryers and see which one(s) work(s) the best.

- Gather up all of your prescription and over-the-counter drugs and check the expiration dates on each bottle. Discard any that are past their expiration date.

- Toss out all pill bottles that don't have labels.

- Blister-pack pills often get separated from their boxes. While the blister-pack itself often contains identifying information as to the type of drug and the expiration date, if you're in doubt, get rid of them.

- Look at creams and ointments and consider whether you actually use them anymore. If you

*M*ake sure to dispose of unwanted medications safely. Flushing them down the toilet can be bad for the environment, and simply tossing them in the trash can be deadly to children and animals. Place unwanted medication in a childproof container, then in another jar, which you should make sure to seal securely. Only then should you put the container in the garbage.

haven't used the arthritis rub you bought when your grandma visited, you probably don't need it.

- If you have six boxes of Band-Aids®, combine them. (But *never* combine bottles of pills.)
- Throw out old, dirty tensor bandages.
- Ladies, pay particular attention to your collection of cosmetics. You should know that the Food and Drug Administration recommends keeping mascara no longer than three months, because bacteria tend to multiply after that period of time. While there are no regulations in place that require the cosmetic industry to set a specific shelf life for cosmetic items, voluntary guidelines show that the stability of cosmetics varies widely after 18 months. This is especially true of "all natural" cosmetics and personal-care products, which may contain plant-derived substances conducive to bacterial growth. So check your cosmetics for changes in color or appearance, and when in doubt, toss it out!
- Suntan lotion and sunscreens do not generally have expiration dates, but it is probably a good idea to toss them after 18 months. Sunless tanning lotions can change color with age, giving you an odd-colored tan. If the color has changed, toss the product. Green tans are not attractive on most people.
- If you have kids, or live with someone who acts like one, you probably experience the tumble of rubber duckies, submarines, goggles, and boats falling off the bathtub ledges every time you take

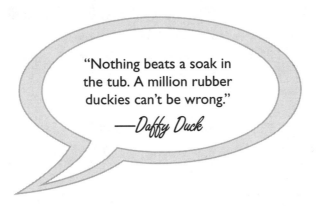

"Nothing beats a soak in the tub. A million rubber duckies can't be wrong."

—*Daffy Duck*

a shower. It's time to pare down the collection and find a dry storage space for the rest in between bath times.

*E*liminate: Now it's time to decide what stays and what goes. Need help? I suggest you throw out:

- Towels and washcloths that have holes, tears, hems coming apart—or have just seen better days—should be put in your rag container.
- Combs with missing teeth, brushes that are falling apart.
- Broken barrettes, elastic ponytail holders that have lost their snap, the hair color (Brigitte Bardot Blonde) that you can't get up your nerve to experiment with.
- If you have magazines dating back three years piling up in a basket beside the throne, it's time to throw out all but the most recent.

- Do you really need to read that bathroom joke book one more time? Now is the perfect time to say good-bye to those knock-knock jokes and create room for necessary storage.

A lot of these items can (and should) just be thrown out. However:

- You probably have a small pile of such things as a dab of nail polish in a bottle, a toothpaste tube with just a little left, some acetone polish remover with a smidgen in the bottom—you get the picture. Relegate the toothpaste and acetone to the cleaning supplies; toothpaste is great for removing grass stains. Toss in that old toothbrush too. Are there some old denture-cleaning tablets lurking in the back of the drawer? Use them to clean your toilet. Use the nail polish to label things. I have three containers of makeup that look the same from the outside. I used red nail polish to

If you have free samples and trial-size toiletries that are taking up space, why not collect them all up and give them to a local homeless shelter?

write the color numbers on the outside in big letters that I can easily see. Take an old container of
clear nail polish and store it in your nylons
drawer or desk drawer to stop runs.

• Sort out the things that can be donated to charity
or sold at a garage sale. Make sure the items are
clean and box them up, putting the garage sale
items in your garage sale staging area and the
charity donation items in a labeled box. You can
not donate medicines or opened cosmetic products. If you found the lotion and bath gel from
your last birthday and never liked the smell, by
all means donate them.

*N*eaten Up: Now look around the room. It's time to
store the essentials. Nearly every area in the bathroom
can be used for storage. Think in terms of walls, doors,
floors, existing cabinets, corners, and even over the
shower and windows.

With your family's traffic flow pattern in mind, look
over the bathroom and determine which areas need
what type of storage. If you style your hair and do
makeup in one area, you'll want to store your tools
conveniently nearby. This same tactic applies to shaving supplies for the men. Since the medicine cabinet is a
poor place to store medicine (humidity is *terrible* for
all medications), let it serve as a storage cabinet for
shaving needs instead.

Those fortunate enough to have a large bathroom will benefit by adding a chest of drawers to the room. Use the largest size you can get away with, and stack towels, linens, and supplies that are not often used. You can paint or decorate the chest of drawers nicely to complement your decor. Just make sure to shellac painted surfaces, so that humidity won't cause paint to crack or peel.

- Consider a tray on the vanity for items such as cotton swabs, cotton balls, deodorants, lotions, and the like. It's far easier to move one tray when cleaning than all sorts of various containers. Look around your own home for cute and different containers. I use a wicker divided chip-and-dip tray, spray painted to match the bathroom, for my cotton balls and Q-tips®.

- Large baskets, serving trays, even glass deviled-egg trays are fun and practical to use in the bathroom for storage. I once bought some beautiful kitchen canisters at a discount store. One of the four canisters was broken, but the three that were intact matched my bath beautifully. I put some cork on the bottom so they wouldn't scratch the marble countertop and stored my styling products in one, swabs and cotton balls in another, and combs belonging to the King and I in the third. I still use them even though they no longer match the bathroom. Now the canisters do storage duty inside enclosed shelves.

- If space is at a premium, attach brackets for shelves to walls over the shower, over the door, or even over the vanity mirror. Also think in terms of plastic or wicker toilet paper holders. They store four or five rolls of toilet paper conveniently. If you have a smart cat, like the Palace Princess, keep her from spinning your toilet paper all over the room by installing it with the paper feed coming from the bottom rather than the top. That way they can't sit and spin!

- Over-the-toilet shelves look nice, but don't often hold much because of the design challenge of fitting over the toilet. A better option is a small corner cabinet that fits over the toilet. Even an étagère (a fancy name for a freestanding shelf unit!) could work well. Remember, the old adage *Out of sight, out of mind* means less cleaning required. That's why I favor cabinets with doors. Baskets inside these cabinets can organize and group things. The baskets can be any style you like—plastic strawberry baskets, wicker, metal, even shoe boxes covered with adhesive-backed paper. Be sure to clearly label the end of the box if contents aren't easily seen. Remember, *Out of sight, out of mind* doesn't give you license to hoard and overbuy. Stay organized. A medicine cabinet is not like a mountain: you don't have to use it *just because it's there.* . . .

- Make use of hooks, over-the-door hangers and over-the-door towel racks. If you have a spot for everybody's towel, there is less likelihood of them ending up in a damp heap on the floor all day. This also lessens the chance of your teenager leaving their damp towel on the bed all day! Smaller children should have hooks and racks that are easily reached.

- Don't forget to add specialty hangers to hold blow dryers and curling irons; these can be found in linen and organizing stores. They attach easily to the wall or inside a cupboard to keep the dryer handy, but neat and out of the way. Or, make your own from an ordinary plastic tubular hanger. Just loop the cord around the bottom bar, twisting firmly until the cord is secure. Tuck the plug into the last few inches of cord for a tight hold.

- Freestanding sinks are great for hiding all sorts of things when you add a decorative skirt with Velcro® tape. The skirt is easily removed for cleaning. In households with children, don't store cleaning chemicals or medicine here; stick to storing things such as blow dryers, hot rollers, or extra toilet paper or supplies.

- Consider adding roll-out shelves to your existing vanity. These shelves are mounted on rollers and pull out, instead of being stationary inside the vanity, so they make items much more accessible

and add up to more for your money, storage-
wise. These shelves also have lips on the end, so
that items don't roll off, which is an unfortunate
hazard with stationary shelves.

• Look for toothbrush holders that are covered
(more hygienic), and try to select one that is dishwasher safe, so that it can be cleaned quickly and
easily. Toothpaste is a good cleaning tool for
many things, but not when it is stuck like cement
all over the toothbrush holder.

Now that your bathroom is so cleverly organized, isn't it
time for a nice bubble bath?

CHAPTER 11

In the Bedroom

*I*deally, a bedroom should be a haven from the workaday world, a retreat where you can relax and let the cares of the day slip away. But that's hard to do if your bedroom is overflowing with clutter! Clothes on the bed, dresser drawers in disarray, and books, magazines, and odds and ends from the rest of the house will all detract from the peaceful atmosphere you want to create in your "room of rest." The important thing here is that this room function for you and your life.

A Little R&R?

Try, if you can, to arrange your room by functions, making sure you have a quiet, uncluttered area for sleeping, as well as space for your other activities. Perhaps a reading section with a cozy chair or lounge and light will appeal to you, or you may want to create a separate nook for a mini-office or a sewing or craft area. It's up to you to designate what your bedroom will be used for, and remember, it only has to be comfortable for you.

Closest to the Closet

Let's begin with the master bedroom, and here we'll talk about storage. The first place we go to store items in the bedroom, of course, is the closet. This is such a big issue I've devoted a whole chapter to it! The thing to remember about the bedroom closet is to keep in there only items that are used regularly—unless, of course, your closet is the size of Imelda Marcos's: she had room for 1,000 pairs of shoes! Most of us don't have that luxury, so for us it makes sense to keep each season's clothes in the bedroom we sleep in, and move out-of-season clothes, hats, purses, and coats to another bedroom closet, the attic, or even the garage. You can purchase metal rolling wardrobe racks for this purpose. Store out-of-season clothing on this and cover with an old sheet or large piece of clean fabric. Place dried citrus peel in the pockets to discourage moths. Remember, don't cover with plastic or store items in plastic dry-cleaning bags. This will discolor them.

Beside the Bedside

Bedside tables with drawers are great, but don't use these as a junk stash. Instead, consider what your needs are. If you like to jot things down while you're reading, for instance, stash paper and pens in your bedside table, as well as night cream, hankies, lip balm, and reading glasses. Another great option for storage is a bedside pocket to hold the book you're reading, extra socks, and a tube of hand cream—things that normally take up space in a drawer or on top of the nightstand. A bedside pocket is quite simply a pocket made of fabric with a longer piece of fabric attached that tucks in between the mattress and box spring. During the day it is covered by the bedspread, and at night it's easily reachable. You can buy these in linen stores or through specialty catalogs, or make your own to match the decor of your room.

For additional storage, consider unfinished round tables. These inexpensive tables work well by the bed, in front of a window, or next to a chair. Usually they come unassembled, with legs that screw in easily to the tabletop. You can cover them with a tablecloth that drapes to the floor. If you are handy, you might make your own covering. I once made a cloth for this type of table out of old ties that belonged to the King. It was a real conversation piece! The cloth hides a wonderful little storage nook underneath. Use yours to store extra linens, bedjackets, or books. Underneath mine I have tucked a box of paperback books that I use for reading material on trips and can leave on the plane or at the hotel when I'm done.

What Goes Where

Small items on top of dressers, chests, and nightstands should be placed on trays or in baskets or decorative hatboxes to keep them contained. Keep display items such as figurines grouped together on a wall shelf or tray on the dresser or counter. Remember, if you don't have a lot of doodads on tops of surfaces, cleaning will go quickly and your room will look restful and less cluttered.

Many of us have additional paperwork we need to store. Try placing a two-drawer file cabinet in the closet, if space permits, or next to a chair. Drape with a tablecloth and voilà! Instant table—and more storage space, to boot!

"If truth is beauty, how come no one has their hair done in a library?"

—Lily Tomlin

Shelves placed over doors or in small unused areas can keep things up off the floor and tabletops. Even small cabinets with doors can be useful when mounted above tables or headboards or placed next to dressers or chests.

What's Hidden Under *Your* Bed?

And let's not overlook that sneaky lode of storage space— underneath the bed. This is a particularly good area to use for out-of-season things such as blankets, comforters, sweaters, seasonal table linens, gift wrapping paper—just about anything you can think of (okay, it's probably not a good spot for that extra honey-glazed ham). I like to label the ends of the boxes or containers so that I don't have to open each one and look through it. Use cardboard or plastic containers; these are readily available at discount stores. Some plastic ones even have drawers that slide out, so that you don't have to pull the entire box out. If you are storing heavy items, plastic boxes will be sturdier for lightweight items, cardboard boxes are fine. If you intend to use storage boxes over an extended period of time, then plastic ones will last longer, so they are a better long-term investment.

Still need more space under the bed? Consider bed risers. These are plastic risers that hold the wheel of the bed frame and raise the bed up 6 or 7 inches. This creates a lot more space under the bed. You can purchase these in sets of four (one for each leg of the bed); double and queen-size beds will take one set, but a king-size bed will require two sets of risers. You can find these in home and health stores or linen catalogs. Do keep in mind that your bed will now be 6 inches higher; so if you are a little short in the legs yourself, you may find yourself literally climbing into bed each night!

The Quick Fix

Don't overlook the quick fixes for storage in your bedroom. I've listed a few to get you started.

- Magazine racks are useful for much more than magazines. Decorate yours to match your bedroom, and fill it with writing materials, fabrics for sewing, or filing that needs to be done.
- Plastic or metal bins can live in your closet or underneath the bed to store out-of-season clothes, books, or gifts.

- Decorative baskets can't be used enough. Great for magazines, extra towels, linens, mini-office or craft supplies, books, and so much more.

- To get the most out of your dresser space, put dividers in drawers for socks and underwear. Roll them instead of folding and they take up less room.

- Assign drawers to suit your needs; if you wear sweaters only occasionally, for instance, put them in a lower drawer. Keep the most easily reached drawers for everyday items.

- A vanity bench is another storage area that can serve a dual purpose. This is your morning "staging area" —especially useful if one or both of you have to make an early exit each day. Use the bench to lay out your clothing the evening before; you can sit on the bench as you dress, then pick up the top to stash small storage items (I use mine to hold my manila folder of monthly bills, believe it or not—it's always in the same place, and I know right where everything is).

- Wooden valets that stand about four feet high with a hanger on top are useful for laying out clothing the night before too. As well as carrying an outfit of clothing, these have a bar across the bottom that holds a pair or two of shoes. When you've finished dressing for the day, you can slip your robe or nightshirt over the valet and place your slippers on the bottom and your nightclothes are ready for you in the evening.

The Guest Bedroom

The guest or spare bedroom is a real lifesaver when you have company, but if it's so cluttered that you can't get to the bed, it won't do you much good. And what about the rest of the time when you have no guests? Then, it's wasted space. This room can be a multipurpose room instead—it's anyone's guess what's in there!

For years the King and I had a lovely big guest room that was occupied almost exclusively by the Palace Pussycat and things we didn't know where else to put. Not only was it wasted space, but I had to clean it out each time we did have guests (which usually meant I was in a hurry), so the pile in the guest room became the pile somewhere else. That wasn't the worst part, though; usually I had to clean it from top to bottom!

- Take a look at your extra room. What is it used for? Does the room now house toys for the kids or serve as a catchall for objects you can't bear to part with (like that StairMaster® you got with such good intentions last year)? Take a good look at your extra room and determine what else it could be used for.

- Most spare rooms are small, but even so they can be converted into mini music studios. These rooms are ideal practice areas to house a keyboard, violin, or other instruments. Keep these in their original cases to prevent damage from exposure to variations in humidity. When storing any of these instruments, be sure they are in a climate-controlled area of your home (not the attic or a damp basement). Properly stored and cared for instruments can be passed on from child to child, thus preserving a considerable investment. An interior walled closet is an excellent storage spot for these instruments; just remember not to stack them, as this may damage sensitive parts like strings or mouthpieces. Cube storage is ideal for musical instruments, since it contains them in one space and they can be lifted in and out of the closet with minimum possibility of damage. This also allows you to store sheet music, extra strings, guitar picks, and so on, with the instrument, so everything is in one place at practice time. When you're paying $30 for a half-hour lesson, time is money and you don't want to scramble around the house looking for the sheet music to Junior's piece for the fall recital! Follow any storage directions that come with the instruments or check with a reputable music store for advice.

• Another fine use of this space is as the hobby or sewing room. Here, a narrow table or small desk along a wall with narrow cupboards or drawers above is ideal. This will allow you to have the items you need to work with right at your fingertips, without the clutter and mess lying around you. A big plus is that you will be able to find what you need without looking through everything.

Guess Who's Coming for... Overnight!

Are you one of those people who say, "When you're in town, be sure you come and visit us?" Well, now is the time to pay up, because guess what—company's coming!

If you're expecting out-of-town guests, you want everything to look its best, especially the room they will be sleeping in. Of course, that means you'll have to have a bed in there! Start by looking at what you've got. A twin bed can be pushed against a wall and outfitted as a daybed very inexpensively. A daybed is actually a bed that masquerades as a sofa/sitting area. You can transform a twin bed into a daybed by placing a fitted coverlet over the mattress and arranging pillows that match across the top. These coverlet sets are found at linen and discount stores. You can still use your twin sheets to make up the bed. Full or queen size beds can also be pushed close to the wall (careful, leave enough room to walk around the bed so you can make it) and the underbed area used for storage of out-of-season clothing, gift wrapping, and so on. Under this bed is also a great spot for oversized items such as seldom-used sports equipment, or even a movie screen. You get the idea.

Before guests arrive, change the sheets and pillowcases. (Don't forget the clean blankets too!) Make the closet look its best by first being sure there is plenty of open hanging space, even if you have to remove some of your stored clothing. Put plenty of hangers in easy reach, including some for hanging trousers and skirts. A few cedar chips or a decorative sachet is a nice touch too. Air the room if it needs it, or spritz with a room spray or homemade air freshener.

Provide some drawer space so that your guests can put away their clothes and store their suitcase during the visit, or provide a luggage rack for this purpose. As a final welcoming touch, do like the classy hotels and tie several spare pillows together like a gift package with ribbon or string. Store them on the closet shelf. This not only looks nice, but also gives the pillows stability, so they will sit on the shelf better, without tumbling out every time the closet door is opened.

Organizing the spare room pays off because it allows you to use every inch of space in your home to the fullest, without stress or fuss. No need to go into panic mode when company calls; you're ready for every occasion!

CHAPTER 12

Go to Your Room

Kids' rooms are often messy, with crayons here, dolls and trucks there, and a teddy bear or two hanging around for good measure. But don't confuse messy with cluttered. Anyone who has put away the crayons, parked the trucks, and put the dolls to bed knows how easy this "mess" can be to deal with—easy, that is, if you don't have clutter. Clutter is that stuff you have to go through *before* finding your daughter's favorite pink T-shirt or your son's favorite baseball mitt. It's three odd socks, an overdue library book, and the beginning of a long abandoned finger-painted masterpiece. And it can be really irritating.

Because children are continuously growing, their rooms are often the easiest in which to

*G*et rid of kids' clutter and you'll be rewarded twice: with an organized kids' room now, and organized kids later!

find items to eliminate. What clothes and toys has your child outgrown? Are the days of infant-sized onesies long gone? Then it's time to throw out the stained and worn, and pass on the good. Now that Susie is five, does she really still need her infant mobile? Pack up those toys your child has deemed no longer interesting and donate them to charity. You may even enlist your child's help. We used to have a rule in my house that for every new toy, one old toy had to be donated to the children's hospital. Knowing that their toys were going to other boys and girls just like them and not the garbage dump helped my son to volunteer toys for donation with minimum hassle. Try it. They may surprise you! But please, no broken toys. These do belong in the trash.

Of course, you will want to keep a few sentimental toys and items of clothing, and some (but not all!) of their artwork. Store these in a plastic bin with a secure lid on the top shelf of their closet.

Storage and Furniture

- First, question what your child's needs are. For preschoolers up to kindergarten age, a toy box and some low shelves for books is all that is really needed.

- As your child grows, he'll need more in the way of storage. Add more shelving; a desk or table with a lamp and chair for schoolwork and projects and space for a computer are all-important.

- Teenagers may need an area for a television and/or stereo set and a phone (and teenage girls will need lots of closet space to accommodate their many trips to the mall!).

- Take a look at the height of your children, and then organize the room accordingly. Keep shelves and hooks low enough for them to reach.

- You might want to hang the hooks just a little above eye level. This will encourage kids to use the hooks and also make them obvious enough to prevent a bumped head.

Next, let's evaluate what you already have and what you need. Look at furniture options that will grow with the kids.

- Beds with storage built in underneath are particularly good, since kids of almost any age can reach them. These beds can take kids to adulthood.

- When purchasing furniture for baby, consider chests and armoires that can be used as the child grows up. This way, there's no need to purchase two sets of furniture!

- Any furniture or shelving used in kids' rooms should be solid and stable. Each piece should hold the weight of a toddler; you know how they climb. If the furniture becomes wobbly or off balance with a 20-pound bag of birdseed or cat litter on it, then it is not safe for your toddler.

- Bookshelves need to be well supported and made of sturdy material. If shelves are freestanding, be certain they are bolted securely to the wall.

Evaluate your child's needs for hanging clothes in the closet.

- Consider installing a temporary closet rod that is low enough that they can reach their clothes (even a shower curtain tension bar will work). Adjust the rod as the children grow until they can use the regular rod.

- Shelves to hold stuffed animals and things that are seldom played with can be at a higher level, leaving lower shelves for books, games, computer discs, and other things.

- When kids are small, consider placing shelves on brackets on the lower closet walls. They can eventually be removed too. This is a great place to store games.

You know the drill by now. Once you've gotten rid of the clutter (good-bye, broken Game Boy®; good-bye, one-legged doll), it's time to Neaten Up. But it's a little different this time. Now you're going to neaten up and organize in such a way as to encourage your children to keep it up for themselves. Think about it. If you pick up your kids things today, you can be darn sure you're going to have to do it tomorrow, and the day after that, and the day after that. . . . Why not teach your children to look after their own belongings? Of course, you'll have to organize their rooms so that it's easy for them to put away their own things. And, of course, you'll have to expect different things from a five-year-old and a fourteen-year-old (the five-year-old is probably going to be much easier to deal with!). But give it a try. You have nothing to lose, and, oh, so much to gain!

Here are some tips to help you organize your children's rooms so they can help keep them organized themselves:

- An over-the-door shoe bag is excellent for organizing not only shoes, but other small pieces of clothing such as socks, mittens, earmuffs, or even toys. Keep the bottom pouches filled with things the kids need to reach; save the top areas for things you can help them with, such as hair accessories and things reserved for special occasions.

- Collections such as stamps and baseball cards can fit nicely on bookshelves. Shoe boxes work well to keep things together, as do inexpensive file-card-size file boxes and clear, clean fast-food containers.

- Blocks can be stored easily in small laundry baskets or plastic bins. Mesh bags are great too.

- Toys with lots of little parts can easily get broken, and the pieces can get mislaid. Try storing small parts in Tupperware® containers or Ziploc® bags. Both come in a wonderful assortment of sizes.

- Larger toys can be stored in toy boxes or chests. Wicker hampers work well too. They are lightweight, with no heavy lids to close on little fingers, and as children grow the wickerwork can be put to work as laundry hampers.

- Dolls and their clothes and accessories can be stored in plastic under-the-bed storage boxes. The accessories won't become separated from the doll, and storage is simple, even for a child.

- Boxed games can be tied shut or have a bungee cord put around them, so that lids don't come loose and contents jumbled.

- A net hammock hung in a corner of the room is great for stuffed animals and other soft toys that don't get played with often but are too precious to give up.

Lost and Found

When I was young, I used one of my grandpa's old cigar boxes as a Lost and Found. Each time I came across a small game piece, an errant dice, or an "anonymous" part of a toy, I just tossed it into the box until I needed it—or figured out what the heck it was! The Queen Mum taught me that, and it saved us hours of searching for lost treasures. You may not have a cigar-smoking grandpa, in which case I suggest you use a shoe box or a big empty chocolate box as your Lost and Found. Try it though. You may never again have to look for the last piece of that jigsaw puzzle again.

Shared Rooms

Shared rooms offer a special challenge. Even though more than one child is living in the room, each child needs an area they can call their own. Even the tiniest members of the household are no exception. So before one of your precious children divides the room in two with the entrance squarely in his half—thereby preventing his younger sibling from coming or going—you need to step in and create areas of the room each child can call his own. You'll be saving your very sanity by following these tips:

- Separate the room. Put a bed on each side and provide individual storage for each child.

- Divide the closet evenly. If necessary, place a temporary vertical partition down the center of the closet and assign each child a side. You can divide the closet easily by tacking a piece of fabric to the shelf and letting it drop to the floor, or you can use a piece of painted lightweight wood that you cut to fit between the shelf and the floor. Assigning each child their own special-colored hangers also helps.

- In a shared room, color identification is helpful. If it's blue storage units or hangers, it belongs to Bob, and if it's red, it belongs to Mike. Color code toy storage areas, closet areas, and other furniture and accessories.

- Provide separate chests of drawers if possible; if not, assign drawers by labeling. Pick up inexpensive unfinished furniture and paint each child's furniture a different color, or divide the drawers by color.

- Teach the children to respect each other's areas, just as if they were separate rooms. It's a good life lesson.

- For a real touch of privacy, hang a lightweight roll-up plastic shade from the ceiling. When pulled down, it is a Do Not Disturb sign. When up, the kids are again happily sharing their area.

The Dreaded . . . Locker

While we're talking about kids, let's have a word about lockers. We all know how they smell . . . gym socks from the start of the school year, an apple from lunch two weeks ago, and how about those gym shoes! They are crammed full of schoolbooks that never make it to class or home, CDs, notes from friends, cookie crumbs, and there may actually be a coat and some gym clothes in there somewhere. Whoever invented the tall, narrow, dark locker knew nothing about kids and clutter. I mean, *come on;* a tiny shelf with three metal hooks and a gaping 6 feet of horror. Back when I went to school, my coat and a couple of pencils and some books fit in there pretty well; although I do remember an ugly fight with a Flutophone® one time. Nowadays kids have laptops and tons of other electronic equipment, so proper storage is essential. Here are some simple ideas to keep the kids clutter-free (and fresh smelling!) during the school year.

- Add a few stick-on hooks to hold purses, keys, gym shoes, cameras—and more.
- Hang up a small mesh bag to take in things like a hairbrush, water bottle, and Discman®.
- Pocket organizers are great—stuff them with those annoying little items that get lost at the bottom of the locker. Plastic see-through pockets are great for at-a-glance organization. Cloth pockets are better for the teenager who values her privacy.

- A couple of magnets on the back wall will hold containers for pencils and pens, and you can even hang a plastic grocery bag to fill with trash and toss out weekly. Put magnets on the back of mirrors too (all teenage girls have bad hair days).

- Grid-type stacking shelves are great for holding not just books, but electronic equipment too.

An organized locker will save you from a bag of who-knows-what at the end of the school year.

You're giving your children a priceless lesson when you teach them early to begin conquering clutter, starting with their own rooms. In doing this, they learn to take control of their own lives too. It's a win-win situation for everyone involved.

CHAPTER 13

Come out of the Closet

*N*ow let's venture into the scariest place of all: the closet. Ever go in looking for clothes to wear and wonder if you'll find the item you really need—or worse still—wonder if you'll ever come out? If empty hangers are hanging all over, crowded racks are causing clothes to wrinkle, and you seem to have to iron everything before you can wear it, well, it's time to conquer the closet. Arm yourself with some logical thinking, a sense of humor, plenty of garbage bags and boxes, and you can conquer clutter in your closet in about the same amount of time it takes you to sit through the latest Hollywood blockbuster at your local multiplex. And not only will you be pleased, but the thrift stores nearby will thank you too.

Now, onward . . . but don't think you need to venture in alone. Why not take the *QUEEN* with you!

Question: *What do I want from the closet? What problems do I have every time I go to the closet to select clothes? Is there an area that constantly frustrates me? Are my blouses all mixed up with my husband's shirts? Are my sweaters bunched up on the shelf or getting shoulder dimples from wire hangers? What about my shoes? Have I ever spent 10 minutes looking for that other brown shoe? Do I hang myself on a purse strap every time I reach for a skirt? What do I need to change so that I can get off to a smooth start in the morning?*

Unpack: To do the job right, you have to take everything out of the closet. If you have some rolling racks, put them to use now. If not, you can utilize the shower rod (provided it's attached firmly to the wall), the bed, and floor. Group the clothes by whom they belong to and into categories—blouses in one pile, skirts in another, slacks in still another. You get the idea.

- Remove everything from shelves and floor, sorting as you go. Make piles of keepers, "not sure," and "get rid of." In the keeper piles, try to group types of clothes together, it will save you time later.

- Clothes that need laundering or dry cleaning should go in a dirty-clothes hamper or dry-cleaning basket.

- Take the time to wash down closet walls thoroughly and vacuum the carpet or wash the floor (that way your favorite silk blouse won't get tangled in a cobweb!).

*E*valuate: Sort clothes, putting "toss" or "donate" items into appropriate containers, such as boxes or trash bags. It's a good idea to use black trash bags so that you or the family can't see your "treasures" departing. Place the clothes you are keeping on the bed or a rolling portable rack.

As you are evaluating each item, consider:

- Does it fit?
- Be tough. If you haven't worn it in a year, you probably won't ever wear it again. If you haven't been a size 6 since high school, move on and eliminate the size 6s.
- Do I need to alter this? How much will the alterations cost?
- How about repairs—can the item be repaired and still be wearable?
- Will shoe polish really take care of that huge scuff mark on the toe of my shoe?
- Give yourself permission to have a pile of "not sure" things. These are things you just can't quite make up your mind about. If, after further consideration, you are still not sure, box them up, label the box with its contents, and date it. In six

months if you haven't revisited any of the items, donate the contents or dispose of it.

- Really consider each item. Where will you wear it? When? If you can't come up with a good answer, say good-bye!

*E*liminate

- Get rid of extra wire hangers. Give them back to your dry cleaner if he will take them; otherwise donate them to a nursing home or toss them.
- Anything mismatched will not likely be missed—throw out mismatched items.
- Look through your "not sure" pile one last time and make any additional judgment calls—be strong!

By now you should have boxes and bags for donating, garage sale, and trash. Remove these from the room, so that you have space to work . . . and no matter now tempting it is, don't look in these containers again. If

*I*f things cannot be fixed, altered, or repaired and be really wearable, then they should be tossed. If the items are salvageable, then keep them, but take care of the problem *before* putting the item back in the closet.

they are full, tape them up and label them with where they go and get the trash bags into the trash... quickly! It's like pulling off a Band-Aid®, it hurts less if you just "do it"!

*N*eaten Up

- Determine hanger type—wire, clip, or plastic. Be consistent. A jumble of wire, plastic, and wood hangers will become tangled and be harder to separate and use—plus it just plain looks better!
- Start rehanging clothes, grouping by color and type.
- If using a double-hung system, hang trousers and skirts on the lower rack.
- Group blouses and shirts by color, and hang them over appropriate pants or skirts (this is called instant dressing!)
- Hang long clothes in areas where they won't tangle with things on the bottom of the closet floor.
- Hang or fold and store sweaters. Sweaters actually do better when folded because they don't stretch. If you prefer to hang sweaters, be sure to use padded hangers to avoid those shoulder dimples. And button them to keep their shape.
- Arrange men's ties on a tie rack or hang over a hanger. (Take a tip from a salesman friend of mine who has a vast collection of ties: after he wears one, he slips it off his neck without untying, and drapes it over a hanger in the closet. His wife has

assembled a half dozen "tie hangers" by color in the closet this way.)

- Replace purses on shelves in your storage area, grouping matching purses and shoes together.
- Use a clear plastic shoe box to capture miscellaneous items such as hairbands, scarves, and belts, and place on the shelf.
- Cover seldom-worn clothes with a cloth cover, or group them together and cover with fabric, such as an old sheet or tablecloth, to keep them clean.
- Be sure you have enough light in the closet. Consider a battery-operated light, or one that "taps" on and off as needed. This helps you to avoid leaving the house in one navy and one black shoe!

A Sentimental Journey

Now you're probably staring at a group of what I call the "sentimental keepers." These are things you don't wear or use, but can't bear to part with—so don't. Make sure they are clean (stains can oxidize over time), and pack them in a box labeled something like "sentimental favorites." Store them away, under the bed, on a top shelf, or in the attic (as long as the temperature there remains fairly consistent). You still have the items, but they're not taking up valuable space in your closet. Who knows, one day when you're baby-sitting the grandkids and run out of ideas, you may grab it for a "dress up" box. Most kids love to play this game.

No More Closet Confusion

Let's talk about storage options in your closet.

- First, consider adding extra shelving. This will give you lots of extra space for those things that you don't use often, but still need to have on hand, like handbags and totes, evening shoes, sweaters, and bathing suits.

- If you store things that tend to tip over or fall off the shelf, such as purses or stacks of sweatshirts, put them in a see-through type container such as a plastic milk crate. You want to easily see from the floor what you are looking for. If you used a closed container, have it labeled in bold print.

- I keep a set of "grab-its" in my closet. These are super-long tongs-like things on a long wooden handle that you can use to reach high above your head. Look for these in home and health stores, and catalogs. They are meant for people who lack mobility, but they're a wonderful tool to keep handy, not only in your closet, but in the kitchen, garage, and even the living room.

- Look your closet over and determine how many long items you have, such as dresses and long skirts, trousers that are hung from the cuff, bathrobes, and long coats. This will help you determine how much of your closet space to allocate to their storage. If you don't wear a lot of long things, then you will only need a small area to store them.

- If you have a lot of blouses, shirts, trousers folded over padded hangers, and other shorter things, consider adding a bar to the closet to instantly double your storage space. You don't have to run it the entire length of your closet; you can break the closet up into "long" and "short" zones. By adding double racks, you can store your slacks on the bottom and coordinating blouses on the top rack. Double racks should be installed at about 82 and 42 inches high to make the most of your closet space.

- Separate your clothing by color and you can grab an outfit at a glance when it's time to get dressed. This method also lets you know what items are in the laundry too. By adding an extra rack, you may have enough space in your closet to store sweaters hanging on padded hangers to keep them wrinkle free (although I still say sweaters are better folded—no stretching).

- No need to hang T-shirts; roll them in drawers to conserve space and deter wrinkles.

- Hooks on the back of the closet door are fine for robes and pajamas.

*T*he King thinks I should wear my dresses longer. About three years longer!

Best Foot Forward

Shoe storage is a big factor in how well you will be able to use your closet. There never seems to be enough floor space, and try as you may, shoes seem to have a life of their own. Years ago, I read in a magazine survey that shoes scattered about on the closet floor are a sign of a "creative mind." I can't tell you how many times that comforted me as I entered my closet and surveyed the whirlwind of shoes scattered on the floor. However, folks, being "creative" isn't all that much fun when you're searching for the mate to your favorite black pump at 5:30 AM! I finally solved this dilemma by adding a shelf for shoes on one wall. This keeps shoes off the floor of the closet, and again, you can see at a glance where the pair you want are kept. If there isn't space for shelving like this in your closet, purchase over-the-door shoe pockets from discount or linen stores and group your shoes together, again by color.

Get It Off Your Chest

Fitting a chest of drawers into your closet will really add space and convenience. They're a terrific place to store socks, underwear, pajamas, T-shirts, and workout clothes, as well as out-of-season items such as sweaters and bathing suits. Don't worry about the appearance of the dresser; you can use a castoff from another room, lug one home from a thrift shop or garage sale, or use Aunt Tilly's that has been gathering dust in the attic. Here's a tip if the dresser drawers smell musty: lay a slice of white bread (yes, it must be white) in a bowl and cover with undiluted white vinegar. Place one in each drawer that smells, close the drawer, and leave for 24 hours. When you open it, the smell should be gone. ODORZOUT™ is also a great odor eliminator. It absorbs stubborn odors, including smoke (in case Aunt Tilly was a smoker).

Don't Hamper Your Efforts

A hamper or a rolling three-section clothes sorter on wheels is wonderful to keep in or near the closet, if space permits. Sort your laundry by lights, darks, and hand washables as you take things off and you'll have a jump on laundry day. Keep a separate basket or nylon or canvas bag handy for dry-clean only clothes and you can easily see when a trip to the dry cleaners is necessary. Rolling sorters are great—they can be wheeled right into the laundry room.

Measure Up!

Here are some basic measurements of things usually found in your closet. (I said *usually*. This doesn't include your sophomore cheerleading uniform or the tiara you wore for your school play!) Keep these figures in mind and you'll find it easy to arrange—and rearrange—your closet. (These measurements are standards set by the American Institute of Architects.)

Did you know a standard hanger is between 17½ and 19 inches wide? You will need to allow a little bit of extra clearance to move the hangers in and out of the closet.

Hanging by the Numbers

Long dresses	69 inches
Robes	52 inches
Regular Dresses	45 inches
Skirts	35 inches
Trousers (cuff hung)	44 inches
Trousers (dbl. hung)	30 inches
Blouses and Shirts	28–38 inches
Men's Suits	38 inches
Women's Suits	29 inches
Coats	50–52 inches
Ties	27 inches (hung on a tie rack or over a hanger)
Dress Storage Bags	48 inches
Travel Bags	41 inches
Garment Bags	57 inches
Hanging Shoe Bags	38–72 inches

Single Rods (height)   66–72 inches

Double-Hung Rods (heights)   82 and 42 inches

When making changes to the rack system or shelving in your closet, make sure you keep these measurements in mind.

As you stand admiring your work, why not grab the camera and take a picture of that beautiful closet? Post it in your newly refurbished family scrapbook, and proudly note the date you finally conquered closet clutter!

CHAPTER 14

Putting a New Spin on the Laundry Room

*I*f you are lucky enough to have a room dedicated to laundry, you know how convenient it can be to have everything well within reach. And you also know how cluttered that laundry room can get. Read on for a few tips on how to make laundry day even less of a hassle.

First, let's get rid of that laundry room clutter. Out with that half-empty box of dye, the mismatched socks, and balls of lint that lurk in the corner of your laundry room. Ditto for the box of hardened laundry detergent. Gather up all the junk and toss it. Give the floor a good sweep and you're ready for business.

First—and perhaps most important—be sure to clear a large enough area to sort the dirty clothes into loads. (Yes, loads—you don't want to just throw a wad of clothes into the wash, or the results can be pretty scary!) Do this by sorting whites into one laundry basket, darks into another, delicates or hand washables into a third. I prefer to sort into baskets instead of on the floor because it keeps the dirty clothes in one place, not to mention makes the laundry room look much neater. If your laundry room is small, sort the clothes in a nearby room where you have space.

- To keep your laundry products in a convenient location, first assess your laundry area. Is there a shelf above the washer and dryer, or can wire shelves be installed in this area?

- A shelf above the washer or dryer is the most logical place for your laundry soap, fabric softener, dryer sheets, and spotters. Cabinets or freestanding storage along a wall work well too.

- Small washers and dryers or stackable units that are kept inside a closet can still benefit from the convenience of shelves. You should be able to squeeze out a foot or two of space to hang shelves from brackets; that's enough room for your basic laundry supplies.

- Remember, when you're thinking about shelves, up high is better than down low. First of all, it's easier to reach for a product than bend over for it, and second, it will keep chemicals out of the reach of animals and children. Just make sure you put the shelf at a height where you are not reaching too high or over your head—that could be more than inconvenient, it could be dangerous. Shoulder height or about 6 inches above shoulder height is just right for most people.

- Line up your prewash spotters, detergent, bleaches, and liquid softener near the washer. Keep your dryer fabric softener sheets near the dryer.

- I keep a special spotting basket on my laundry shelf. This is just a plastic basket the size of a shoe box where I keep my more unusual spotters, such as meat tenderizer, rust remover, nongel toothpaste, and commercial spotters. That way, when I need one of these unusual (but very effective) products, I just reach for the basket instead of rummaging around on the shelves.

- I also keep a small sewing kit in my spotting basket for making quick repairs before washing an item. (Small tears can grow in the washing machine.)

- No shelves or cabinets? Keep all of your washing supplies in a plastic laundry basket, so that you only need to reach in one place for what you need. (Plastic is better here than wicker—spills can be wiped up easily.)

- A shower curtain tension rod hung over the washer and dryer can make laundry day easier. If your wall space is too far apart to use a tension rod, you can use a pole-type curtain rod and attach it to the walls.

- Bring empty hangers from the closets on laundry day and hang them on the rod. As clothes are removed from the dryer, they can be hung immediately, so that much less ironing time is required. This also aids in sorting clothes for a quick return to the right closet.

- An over-the-door hanger is a good option if space is too tight in your laundry room for a tension rod. Keep some spare hangers here and hang clothes as you sort things out of the dryer.

- A miniature-sized wastebasket on top of your dryer is handy for cleaning the lint screen after each load, it's also a great visual reminder to do that often-forgotten job. A quick and easy way to clean this screen is to swipe it with a used dryer fabric softener sheet. Lint is picked right up and deposited in the trash neatly—no muss, no fuss. Keep an old tissue box nearby where you can store these "retired" sheets for this purpose.

- Don't overlook any storage space between the washer and dryer. Take advantage of it with a narrow rolling cart to store your laundry supplies.

- Some folks love to iron (I only like to talk about it, but I have a friend who swears it's therapeutic). If you do a lot of ironing and have the room, install an ironing board that folds flat against the wall and drops down when you're ready to use it. The iron can be stored on a shelf above where the ironing board is mounted, in a cabinet, or on the shelf with your cleaning supplies.

- No room in the laundry room, but still need an iron and ironing board handy? Consider an inexpensive

*I*f you're like me and use retired fabric softener sheets for dusting, removing burned-on food from casseroles, and keeping your sewing thread from tangling, why not keep them handy in an old tissue box on your laundry room shelf?

over-the-door ironing board holder in a nearby bedroom or den. This keeps the ironing board ready for
use at a minute's notice.

Basement laundry rooms tend to get clothes scattered all
over the floor. There are some creative solutions for this:

- If your home is an older one, you may very well own
  a laundry chute, where family members can toss their
  dirty clothes into a "black hole." Capture those
  clothes when they tumble down by using either a
  portable crib (very handy, as the sides are mesh and
  plastic, and these are resistant to dampness and
  mildew) or a large plastic trash barrel. Keep several
  empty laundry baskets nearby for sorting at laundry
  time.

- If your family tosses their clothes into the laundry
  room on a regular basis, have some baskets labeled
  (and color-coded) for whites, darks, and delicates.

- If you wash a lot of jeans, then be sure to label a basket just for those. That will start your sorting process
  before you want to start the laundry.

- When laundry rooms are located a little ways from
  the living areas of the house, such as in a basement or
  garage, it's easy to forget when a load has finished
  washing or drying. Solution? Set your kitchen timer
  or purchase a small timer to ring when it's time to get
  the clothes. This will save many a wrinkle, and speed
  up the process too.

- Last but not least, if you fold clothes on the washer and dryer or keep detergent boxes sitting on it, consider covering the top of your appliances with a towel to protect the finish from wear and tear. Sooner or later setting things on top of the appliances will remove the finish, and once the finish is gone, the rust can begin.

- Just because this is a place for washing clothes doesn't mean your laundry room should be dark and drab. You can add a throw rug (careful that it has a nonskid bottom) and a few pictures. One artist friend of mine even stenciled a beautiful garden scene in her laundry room; she figured she spent so much time in there she might as well enjoy it. The laundry room was the brightest and most cheerful spot in the whole house!

Hitting the Road with Your Laundry

If you travel to the Laundromat® or an apartment building laundry room, you will have special concerns. There are ways to make the job easier:

- Sort your clothes by loads into plastic bags before you leave home. Tall kitchen trash bags or plastic grocery bags work well for this. You can use the kitchen trash bags over and over. Pop the bags into a laundry basket, rolling bag, or whatever you transport your laundry in.

- Consider switching from liquid or powder detergent to the laundry tabs. You can drop them right in the bag as you sort the clothes, and you won't need to carry your laundry detergent with you.

- Put dryer sheets in a resealable plastic bag to avoid carrying the bulky box.

- Powdered bleach can also be carried in a resealable bag along with an appropriate-size measuring cup.

- Wire or nylon carts on wheels are handy for transporting the laundry and supplies to the laundry area. Look for ones that are collapsible and can be hung up when not in use. Of course, this will be appropriate only for those of you who have a laundry in your building. People who have to cart their laundry a couple of blocks might find a shopping buggy useful for hauling those large loads.

- Don't forget to bring your hangers, and use twist ties to hook together the hangers holding freshly hung clothes. The hangers won't become tangled or separated and will be easier to transport.

Once you get the hang of it, airing your dirty laundry isn't half bad. Follow these simple methods and you'll be onto something a lot more fun before you know it.

CHAPTER 15

Flowers in the Attic

*O*kay, so nobody really has flowers in the attic. It's not a place to be prettied with up with bouquets and doilies, and it's not a place for entertaining. But that doesn't mean your attic should hold piles of clutter either. Do you really want to fill up this premium real estate with broken furniture, long-forgotten board games, and your aunt Esther's collection of teaspoons from all the state capitals? It doesn't have to be that way.

An attic can be a great storage area as long as you keep in mind a few simple precautions and follow a few simple rules. Most important, take the time to *eliminate*. Remember: The goal is to conquer clutter, not just move it around the house. Why pack up unwanted items and then put them in the attic (or the basement or the garage) when you can deal with them once and for all? Eventually, everything that is packed is going to have to be unpacked. So why spend precious time dealing with "stuff" when you could be out enjoying yourself, spending time with your family, or working on a hobby that you really enjoy?

Remember that its radical shifts in temperature make the attic an unsuitable choice for storing many climate-sensitive items. Bugs can also be a problem, so make sure to keep insects and other pests away by spraying the attic well with a good, all-purpose, preferably poison-free organic bug spray. Pay spe-

*D*on't make clutter your hobby.

cial attention to the floor and baseboard areas. It's a good rule of thumb to vacuum the attic area down at least once a year. You might also want to try some of my own concoctions to keep bugs away:

- A mixture of 50 percent confectioner's sugar and 50 percent 20 Mule Team® Borax placed on a piece of cardboard in corners of the attic will make sure that ants feast and die. Remember, kids and pets should not ingest this mixture.

- Cockroaches can be eliminated with a mixture of 50 percent boric acid added to 25 percent nondairy creamer and 25 percent sugar. Sprinkle this mixture behind the stove and refrigerator and under the sink at the back of the cupboard. The roaches will ingest this and die. Keep this out of the reach of children and pets.

- For moths, skip the smelly mothballs, and instead, dry strips of citrus peel overnight in an oven you have warmed to 200 degrees and then shut off. Sprinkle them around clothes and into pockets of stored clothes for excellent moth protection.

Now remember, not everything can be stored safely in the attic. Follow these *do's* and *don'ts*.

DO Store the Following in the Attic:

- Dishes and pottery
- Holiday decorations
- Housewares
- Clothing—with some exceptions

DON'T Store the Following in the Attic:

- Blankets
- Stuffed animals
- Leather goods
- Fur coats

*I*tems likely to be affected by moisture and extremes in temperature should not be stored in the attic.

Let's Start with the *Do's*

- Surplus crockery should be wrapped in tissue and packed in a cardboard box. Throw in a handful of dried citrus peels to eliminate that musty odor.

- Seasonal decorations are perfect for the attic. Just make sure to store them in cardboard boxes (not plastic) to eliminate moisture buildup and avoid the possibility of mold and mildew.

- Specialty housewares such as the cake pans used for holidays and birthdays, the punch bowl with twelve matching cups, and the centerpiece you use at Easter can safely stay in the attic. Ditto for canning jars and equipment used to preserve fruits and vegetables. (Note: Don't store the rubber rings for canning in the attic, as the temperature fluctuations will cause them to dry and crack. A pantry shelf is a better option for these.)

- Winter coats, hats, scarves, mittens, and the like can be stored in the attic. So can baby dresses and com-

*R*emember to check on clothing stored in the attic at least every six months for any damage. Make a note to do this on your kitchen or office calendar.

munion dresses. Just make sure you follow a few simple precautions:

- Make sure the clothing is dry-cleaned or washed prior to storage. Food stains are often invisible to the naked eye, but they attract moths.
- Don't store your clothes in plastic bags or drop cloths; this can discolor them.
- Fine clothes should be wrapped in tissue paper.
- Hang your clothing on a portable rack, or suspend a clothesline from the rafters and use plastic hangers.
- Allow enough space between items for air to circulate.
- Cover with a clean, light-colored sheet. (In unpredictable temperature conditions, dark-colored sheets could stain your clothes.)
- And don't forget to scatter citrus peels or cedar chips. (They smell much nicer than mothballs, and work just as well at deterring pests.)

*T*o dry rinds for moth repellent, peel oranges, lemons, limes, or any other citrus fruit into strips about ½ inch wide. Heat the oven to 200 degrees and turn off. Spread the peels in a single layer on a clean cookie sheet, and leave in the closed oven until the peels are dried—usually overnight.

- Toys can easily be stored in the attic by placing them in a cabinet or box, or covering them with a plastic drop cloth or sheet. Keeping toys covered will mean less cleaning when it's time to use them again. Make sure all parts are in one place before toys are stored.
- Seasonal sports equipment such as golf clubs, skis, bikes, balls, tennis rackets, bowling balls, and so on can also be stored in the attic.
- Consider using a large plastic trash can to hold rackets, bats, mallets, and hockey sticks. This keeps things neatly contained in one place.
- Tennis balls, footballs, and soccer balls can be kept in a smaller plastic trash can.
- Golf balls and tees can be stored together in a clear plastic shoe box with a lid for easy identification. Or try storing them in mesh laundry bags hooked on the wall.

Remember that items stored in the attic are out of sight and frequently forgotten, so make a list of the equipment on hand in the attic. This way you can easily retrieve items and also save yourself from needless expenditures if Junior decides he wants to take up tennis or golf.

And Now the *Don'ts*

- Blankets, stuffed animals, leather items, and fur coats and stoles should not be stored in the attic. They're an open invitation for rodents to build a nest.

- Store blankets folded away in an underbed box or a top shelf in a closet.

- Stuffed animals should be sorted out occasionally; give those you don't need to a favorite charity. Clean stuffed animals by placing in a large plastic garbage bag with a few shakes of baking soda. Tie bag closed and shake, then remove toys. Brush them thoroughly to clean off baking soda. When you're done, just throw the bag away.

- Fur coats and stoles that have seen better days can be made over into stuffed teddy bears. Do an Internet search using keywords "recycled fur coats" for more details.

- Your attic is not the place for storing temperature-sensitive items such as CDs, books, tapes, important papers, your family photo albums, cameras, or electronic equipment. Store these things close to or in the rooms they're used in.

How to Store

You may want to install shelves in the attic and store dishes on these, covered with a plastic drop cloth. This will keep dust from collecting and make it easy to see at a glance what you have. Consider putting some old kitchen cabinets in the attic. They make great storage areas for dishes and other similar items, and your crockery will stay much cleaner when stored in an enclosed area.

Label each box carefully, so you can take down only the

boxes you want. I always tape a file card to the top and write down a list of what's inside. Keep a separate card that lists anything that might need repair before you use it, like a string of lights that doesn't work. It's an especially good idea to store all Christmas light replacement bulbs in one container; a plastic one with a lid is best. By doing this, you won't find yourself digging through the house on Christmas Eve, looking for that replacement bulb for your angel on top of the tree. Tree skirts and fabric pieces should be stored in boxes as well. Wrap them in tissue first and label the boxes for easy identification.

And, yes, you really can store flowers in the attic. Just make sure they're made of plastic or silk. Dust or clean them thoroughly before covering with an old sheet and labeling for easy reference.

CHAPTER 16

Going Down Under

G'day, mate! Going down under can be fun, unless you are referring to the basement. Basements tend to collect all of the clutter and stuff that you don't know what to do with. It just seems easier on cleaning day to grab what doesn't belong or is taking up space and stash it in the basement to be dealt with later. And let's face it, later rarely comes.

Most basements accumulate the stuff that we just can't bear to part with or don't have time to make a decision about. Over time, all of this excess clutter from the rest of the house fills the basement, robbing it of space for *useful* storage. The time has come to question what your basement requires in order to become more user-friendly and a great storage or play area. And where there's a question, there's a *QUEEN*:

*Q*uestion: *What purpose do I want the basement to serve? Is it to be given over completely to storage? Is there room here for the kids to play, or for hobbies and* crafts? *How do I want to make use of this space—and who is going to use it?*

*U*npack: This step is vital in the basement, since many things may have been boxed and stored there for perhaps years. Many of us who have moved several times have had this experience. After a move, three or four boxes are still filled with items that don't fit the new home and somehow end up in the basement. It's time to open those boxes and make a decision. If you can use the orange throw pillows or the Early American clock in your home, fine. If not, they go to charity. As you unpack, dispose of boxes that are not usable for storage again and get them out of your way, so that you have space to work.

*E*valuate: Let's take a good look at your basement. Is there an old rocking chair with a broken seat, a pile of mildewy cushions from a patio set you no longer own, and a kitchen table minus the legs? Take stock of what you have and what you need. If they're not the same, move on to the next step. . . . During this process, evaluate the condition of your basement too. If you have leaks or other problems, this is a good time to make repairs.

*E*liminate: If you don't do it now, you never will. If you haven't missed anything in those boxes since your last move, get them out of there. They are taking up precious storage space. Get rid of broken items, rusty items, anything you really don't need. When you buy a house with a basement, you don't sign a commitment to fill it up with clutter from everywhere else.

This means it's time to actually open every box and determine whether you need what is in it. If there's something stored in the basement that you haven't looked for in more than a year, eliminate it. Donate it, move it to the garage sale pile, or trash it.

Break down any empty boxes that contained electronic equipment that must be returned in its original carton for repair. Since your warranty requires that you save them, store the now-flat boxes tied together in one area.

When you're evaluating the basement, you have to do more than evaluate your clutter—you have to evaluate the basement itself, because moisture is often a problem in basements, and it's easier to prevent mildew than combat it once it begins.

*W*hile you're decluttering the basement, take the time to move the washer and dryer and check for leaky or broken hoses. Try to do this every six months.

- Portable dehumidifiers are a must in some areas. They're great at pulling excess humidity out of the air. The water collected from these is excellent for plants because it is pure, so save it to do your watering with. Keep an empty watering can or bucket nearby to transfer the water.

- Control mildewy odors by placing bowls of dry ODORZOUT™ around the basement, changing the bowls until the odor disappears. Wintergreen oil (available at the health-food store) is another wonderful deodorizer. Saturate cotton balls with the oil and place in strategic areas to combat odor.

- In areas prone to flooding, or in houses with water seepage problems, investigate whether a sump pump may control it. Once water is detected, the sump pump will turn on and immediately start removing the water. Remember that the floor area of a damp basement is not a good storage area for much of anything. Clothes will mildew, cardboard boxes will fall apart, and even

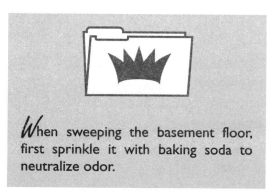

*W*hen sweeping the basement floor, first sprinkle it with baking soda to neutralize odor.

items stored in plastic boxes will take on a pungent odor from the excess humidity. So don't even try to use this as a storage space. You'll want to keep the floor area cleared out as much as possible in case of flooding or seepage.

*N*eaten Up: I always like this part best. It means you are almost done and you'll see results soon. A basement can be home to all kinds and types of storage. You can use anything and everything as storage units. Be imaginative. Look around the house, the garage, and the basement to see what you are not using efficiently, and use it for basement storage permanently.

- A closet with shelves in a basement can house a number of things. Salvaged kitchen cabinets and freestanding units such as old filing cabinets or armoires work too. Your storage options here don't have to be fancy to work.

- Sturdy coated-wire shelving is also a good choice. Here you can place items such as extra paper products, lightbulbs, or household goods in their packaging, to bring upstairs when needed. Remember to store other items on these shelves in containers, for easier cleaning.

- Keep items off the floor when storing in the basement. Start shelves and cabinets a foot or so off the ground. This will help keep dampness away from your belongings, and if you ever have a

basement flood, heaven forbid, your possessions
should be high and dry.

- Hanging things from wall pegboards is another
good option. This provides storage for tools,
extra pots and pans, and toys. Organize like items
together, grouping several pegboards in a row if
need be. Don't forget to check tools for rust
occasionally.

- A basement is not the place to store books, photos,
good wood furniture, or fabrics that can be dam-
aged by moisture. And it's definitely not the spot
for your family heirlooms or photo albums, either.

- Think "outside the box" with your basement. In
locales with long winters or rainy seasons, this
might be an ideal spot for a Ping-Pong® table, a
StairMaster®, or even a wall-mounted television set
with a mat, for following those yoga tapes you've
collected. Basements also make ideal hobby and
craft areas. You can purchase an old wooden
kitchen table and use it to assemble a birdhouse,
learn how to rubber-stamp, or tie-dye a bedspread.

Back when we were kids, we often called the basement the rum-
pus room. With today's hectic lifestyles, it's a relief to retreat to
a room that's ready for some no-frills fun. Basements can be
great stress relievers when the gang gets together for a silly game
of Twister®, a craft project, or even a game of beanbag tag. And
with all the clutter out of the way, who knows, you may even
get to enjoy going "down under"!

CHAPTER 17

The Outer Limits

*I*s your garage loaded with broken, outgrown, unused toys and sports equipment? Are there empty containers of car wash soap, fertilizer, and pesticides taking up space? Could it be you have parts to things you don't even own anymore lying around? It's time to spruce up the garage.

Start by moving cars out of the garage, and then begin moving what is left. Use your driveway to group items together. You should come up with a few collections like this:

- Sporting equipment (golf clubs, bats, balls, tennis rackets, hockey sticks)
- Power tools—this means anything with a cord (okay, maybe not venetian blinds!)
- Regular tools
- Lawn equipment such as rakes, hoes, and clippers
- Snow shovels and blowers

- Patio furniture
- Pool supplies

Dispose of the obvious junk, like old bicycle tires, empty boxes, and dirty rags. To dispose of pesticides safely, follow the directions on the container. Some things, such as motor oil, solvents, and garden chemicals, cannot simply be tossed in the trash. Check with the company that collects your trash, and they will give you the guidelines for your state.

Once you've cleared out the clutter, you may be left with a pile of "not sures." These could be things that need repair or something that you were going to salvage usable parts from.

You know it's time to declutter the garage when you don't have room for the car!

Now is the time to determine whether these things are worth saving. You can box and label them and if you haven't used them in another six months, trash them, or you could take the time now to remove the parts you want or to repair what needs it, and you're done. If you still have some not sures, the six month rule applies—if you haven't looked at it or used it in six months, it's out of there, no excuses!

Now that you've got the garage clear (for the first time in how many years?), why not take the opportunity to clean the floor. First sweep out all loose debris, and then mix up a bucket of hot water with some trisodium phosphate or your favorite degreasing cleaner. Wash the floor well, using an old mop, and pour the solution on, scrubbing it in with a broom. Rinse the floor well and let it dry before you start to neaten up.

It's a good idea to mark off the area that is occupied by the car or cars in your garage, so that you can visualize what storage areas are remaining. Consider the area required for opening car doors and maneuvering the car into and out of the garage. I used a piece of sidewalk chalk to mark off this space before I started.

Stow It Safely

- Decide where you can hang closed cabinets and shelving, keeping in mind that anything stored on open shelves will quickly become soiled. Consider recycling old kitchen cabinets or checking for some at yard sales. In my neighborhood, one new homeowner who didn't want the garage cabinets that came with the house gave them away free; the only catch was their new owner had to come pick them up, which he gladly did.

- Make sure you know the width of the area that you are working with so that you don't end up with shelves hanging over the area the car uses.

- If you put closed shelves at the end of the garage, you can place them high enough that you can still pull the car in underneath them. Because the shelves are closed, items will not fall out and damage the car.

These cupboards are great for sports equipment. You can even dedicate one cupboard to each sport, to keep like items grouped together. This makes it easier to get out the door on time on practice day.

- Keep one cupboard locked at all times and store in it poisonous items such as pesticides, herbicides, and dangerous tools. Keep the key in the house in a safe location.

- Large outdoor toys, lawn equipment, and patio furniture can be stored in an outdoor shed. This avoids having dirt tracked into the garage and house. If you don't have a shed, set up a corner of the garage for the lawn equipment, keeping it as far from the house access as possible and close to the garage door. This will contain the dirt in one place, and you can easily sweep it out the door.

- Place recycling containers in the garage in an area convenient to the door of the house.

- Store garden tools in a plastic 5-gallon bucket or old paint container filled with sand, to keep them clean and free of rust. Keep this near the garage door.

- Hang rakes, large shovels, and garden hoses from hooks on the wall.

- In a garage you always want to "look up." Using the garage walls and ceiling will almost double your garage space. You can build a rack that hangs from the garage ceiling to hold folding tables, chairs, luggage, and other large or unwieldy items. The employees in your local home center's building department should be able to show you how to do this. When hanging a rack from the ceiling, just remember to make sure that it is fastened properly—either to a stud or by using anchors—so that it will bear the weight of the items stored in it. (Of course, I prefer a stud!) You can also purchase ready-made racks at home centers.

- Use ceiling hooks to store bikes during the winter.
- Wall hooks can hold such things as ladders, snow shovels, brooms, and other large tools.

Re-Tool Your Tool Bench

- Tools strewn all over the workbench make it hard to get the simplest job done. First, you'll want to pick up the entire area and place everything on a bench, table, or floor conveniently nearby. Then, sort out tools according to use and place back on the bench.
- Look for a toolbox made of heavy-duty plastic. These are preferable to metal boxes, which will rust if left on a damp garage floor.
- Consider using pegboard or tool racks to hang tools over or next to the workbench too. Trace the outline of the hammers, pliers, rope, and so on, with chalk or marker so you can easily see what tool goes where.
- Install a small shelf over the workbench and arrange your containers of nails, screws, nuts, and bolts on the shelf. Or use clear plastic containers and hang from the walls. For storage, use old coffee cans, mar-

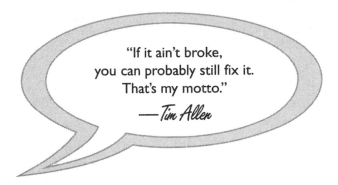

"If it ain't broke,
you can probably still fix it.
That's my motto."

—Tim Allen

garine tubs, or empty plastic containers. Just make sure to label them clearly, so that you don't have to fish around every time you want to find a finishing nail.

And Don't Forget

- Keep the area where you walk clear. If you have a garage service door leading outside, keep a path clear that you can use.

- Keep the area around the door leading to the house clear of things and clean. A good walk-off mat will keep you from tracking in debris.

- Consider establishing an area where you and your family can remove dirty shoes and boots before you enter the house.

- Carports or decks can also be outfitted with extra storage space by using wall hooks and ceiling racks for lawn equipment, tools, and patio furniture. Investigate purchasing a shed for the backyard to store your large outdoor items when not in use. This can be arranged just like a mini-garage.

Stand back and take a look at your efforts. I bet the neighbors are looking enviously at your garage too. Now the next time it rains or snows, you can run out to the garage and hop in the car, where it sits high and dry, instead of racing to the driveway where you used to have to park. A clutter-free garage is a great thing!

It's tempting to use glass containers such as old baby food jars to store small items, but don't! When they break, you can have shards of glass scatter all around your tools, not to mention on the garage floor, where it can easily puncture a tire.

CHAPTER 18

Do Your Homework

Whether you run your entire business from a home office or have just designated an area to handle work at home, the goal should be the same: create a quiet, clutter-free, stress-free environment where you can accomplish a lot in a short amount of time.

A messy, cluttered office may cause you to miss deadlines and lose information, not to mention get on your nerves. I mean, who wants to waste time looking for phone numbers when there's work to be done? Here you need to evaluate the use of your office and desk area and then make it work for you rather than against you. I've put together a few suggestions for getting yourself clutter-free and organized, but jump right in and use your imagination . . . after all, it is *your* office, so there are no rights or wrongs.

When you have a home office, it seems to be a clutter magnet. Sometimes it is in a multipurpose room, and you end up moving the sewing you need to work on later in order to balance your checkbook now. If you want to sit down and work on your novel, the mood will be gone and, trust me, so will the ideas if you have to clear a place to work. You waste precious time just looking for a place to work and another place to put all the things that are in the way. For your office to function, it needs to be properly located and have designated areas for everything.

Where to Work?

Interruptions will decrease your productivity and cause you to spend more hours working. Make sure the area you work in has a door that can be closed when it's time to go to work. A closed door means Do Not Disturb. Remember that people who work at home successfully learn to establish regular business hours and stick to them. Otherwise, they find themselves working seven days a week, many hours per day.

Here are some suggestions on choosing a designated working area in your home:

- The basement might be suitable, and certainly it might be quiet and away from the kids, but watch out for dampness, which can damage sensitive electronic equipment. A good dehumidifier is a must if you live in a damp area. Keep computers and other equipment up off the floor, and position outlets at least a foot off the floor as well. Basements can be rather drab, so you'll want to use light, bright colors to create a feeling of cheeriness. Investigate installing overhead track lights as well as good lighting near your work area to decrease eyestrain. A friend who runs a home business from her basement keeps a mini trampoline and jump rope close by. Every hour or so, she skips rope or bounces around for a few minutes. Great stress relief—and gives those tense back and neck muscles a change of pace too!

- A guest room can work well—when you don't have guests, that is. If you have a lot of weekend visitors, you might want to rethink setting up in an area that will frequently be occupied by other people.

- The family room is not a good choice because it's centrally located and noisy. Ditto for the kitchen. You can have a desk or counter area in the kitchen for bill paying and coupon clipping, but trying to work quietly in the hub of the home will be an exercise in frustration for you.

- If you are using a shared room or if space is a major concern, consider the advantages of turning a closet into a home office. This can be done quite simply by inserting a desk into a closet. Just make sure to measure the space before you make your purchase. A do-it-yourself desk can be as simple as a laminate board sitting on a pair of two-drawer file cabinets or an old table. Install hanging shelves and a bulletin board to help you organize your daily work. If you are creating one of these areas, look for computer carts that hold everything. Slide one into a closet and pull it out when you need it.

- With the luxury of a little more space, you can still hide your home office behind sliding doors at one end of a room. You can have these installed quite easily; check at your local home center for details. When you're done working, just slide the doors closed and the office is out of sight, so that the room can revert to its other use. Out of sight, out of mind.

You Want to Put It Where?

There is no right or wrong storage container for use in your office. If it works for you, it is exactly the right one; if it doesn't, it doesn't matter how cute, practical, or professional it is—it's wrong.

Get creative and have some fun here. I've used a wicker chip-and-dip tray (the divided areas house paper clips, pens, and Post-it® notes) on my desk for years.

- Divide the drawers of your desk into functional areas for pens, pencils, paper clips, staples, and other necessities. Purchase plastic or metal dividers, or make your own with small boxes or discount store finds.

- Wicker baskets with handles make great carryalls to hold computer discs and CDs.

- Stash small books and pads of paper in square metal kitchen containers from the dollar store. A friend uses an old Barbie® thermos bottle she found at a thrift store to hold pens, pencils, and letter openers.

- Purchase new or used two- or four-drawer file cabinets, or use cardboard banker's file boxes with lids.

Store files that you don't use more than once a year in the attic or basement, so that you will have more space for current things in your office files. Label drawers clearly, so you can quickly find what you need. You can also buy file boxes made of wicker and plastic, most of which have rails built in for hanging folders.

- Don't combine work files with home files.

- Keep a separate drawer for warranties, receipts, and instructions. Divide your files into categories such as *electric, water, cable, Visa®, American Express®,* and *car.*

- As you pay the bills, promptly file the receipts with the most current receipts at the front of the file.

- Keep folders for appliances and other purchases. Keep the instruction booklet and the receipt and any other information you may need in this file. You should have files that are labeled *washer, dryer, TV, stove, refrigerator,* and so on. As you throw out, donate, or replace an item, remove that instruction booklet or attach it to the piece you give away.

Conquer Computer Clutter

Take a few moments now to organize your computer files, and get rid of as much computer clutter as you can. Write down your e-mail passwords on a Rolodex® or index card and store in a handy place nearby. Include the 800 number of the technical support team for the Internet service provider you use. This way you can flip right to the card and the information you need is right at your fingertips. And consider the following to conquer that calamitous computer clutter:

- Many of us receive a barrage of e-mails from well-meaning friends—jokes, current events, craft lists, and so on. Review these e-mails regularly, and if you're getting too many, one polite little e-mail should be enough to stop the flow. You might want to try something like this:

> *As much as I like receiving these fun messages, I'm afraid that I'm just inundated with e-mails. Please remove me from your mailing list. I'll just have to trust that you'll keep me up-to-date next time we get together. Thanks for understanding.*

- Regularly review your e-mail freebies. Remember, it's not free if you have to take your free time to weed through it. How to gauge if enough is enough? Consider this:
  - Do you still receive special offers on maternity clothes, even though your youngest is in the second grade?
  - Are you getting three "joke of the day" e-mails? How many times can that chicken cross the road, anyway?

• Do you still belong to the Hamburger Helper®
   recipe club, but you've been a vegetarian for the
   past three years?

You get the idea. Now you'll have more "surf time" and
less "cleanup time" when you log on.

Use things that work for you. It is your office, and the most
important person to please is yourself!

CHAPTER 19

Getting It All Together

The Queen Mother always told me to wear clean underwear just in case I was in an accident. Think of this as the same thing. You should always have your legal papers together and keep your family informed of the location of these documents in case of emergency. It's not morbid, and it's not tempting fate. It's just being prepared.

Keep your estate-planning documents in order, no matter how old you are. I know this seems scary—who wants to be reminded that life is short?—but it's important to protect your family and ensure that your property is handled the way you want it to be.

Having files stored on the computer is not enough. You should have backup hard copies of your will, power of attorney documents, medical insurance, and tax returns. Specific medical wishes should also be carefully spelled out: write them down and give them to the person you've designated to be your medical power of attorney. Your medical power of attorney documents should also be filed with your doctors. You should be sure that you do this every two years, or as things change. Keep the people who need to know informed of any changes. They'll thank you for it.

Store your hard copies in a fireproof box or a bank safe deposit box. Sit down and go over all of this with your family so that they clearly know your wishes and where your papers are. As part of your documents, keep records of the following information:

- Clergy name and phone number.
- Trusts, including what type, and your adviser.
- Real estate, including type, address, mortgages, bank where mortgage is held and its due date.
- Bank accounts, with bank's full name, address, telephone number, and account numbers.
- Life insurance policies, including the company name, policy number, type of policy, cash value, and the name and phone number of your agent.
- List of any 401Ks or IRAs, including account number, agent, and phone number.
- Military service information: branch, dates of service, rank, status of any pension earned, and death benefits.
- List any debts that you have. Include in this list the names of people and companies/organizations you owe money to, amounts, phone numbers, and where the original loan papers are kept.

- Social security documents and pension information.

- Death instructions: whom to call, name of funeral home, your personal wishes concerning burial information, and paperwork if you own a gravesite.

- Don't forget to include a list of persons to be contacted upon your death. Include addresses and phone numbers.

- Organ donors should make sure that they are identified on their driver's license, that the person designated to be their medical power of attorney is aware of their decision, and that family and friends are informed.

"I filled out an application that said, 'In case of emergency notify . . .' I wrote, 'Doctor.' What's my mother going to do?"

—*Steven Wright*

Make copies of your will to keep at home, but remember, only the original can be probated.

The IRS suggests that tax records be retained for three years. If you own property, keep your returns for as long as you own that property, so that when you sell it, you will know what you paid for it. Tax returns can be safely stored at home.

A quick review:

- Keep a list of where your will, power of attorney, medical power of attorney, and other important documents are stored, and make sure to give copes of this list to family members.
- Keep a list of your assets and liabilities, and be sure to update it as needed. Store this list with your important documents.
- Make a list of the names of your attorney and other legal advisers, and give a copy to family members. Keep another copy in a safe place.
- Put the name of the person who will settle your legal affairs and business on the signature card for your bank safe deposit box so that your affairs can be promptly attended to.

I know this is not fun to talk about, but it will give you peace of mind to have everything in order. This is one of the most loving acts you can perform for your family and friends.

CHAPTER 20

The Last Word

$\mathcal{S}$ome years ago, a modernist architect who was known for his simple, unornamented style coined the phrase, *Less is more.* This certainly applies to staying organized in your home. If you don't accumulate clutter, you won't have to get rid of it.

This is a wonderful theory, but how to put it into practice sure puzzles a lot of us. With the dizzying array of items available to purchase today, it's only natural to feel at times overwhelmed by "stuff." That's why clutter control starts with your purchasing decisions. Here are some things to think about before you shop:

- Think before you buy. Do you really need that? Some questions that may suggest this item is nice, but unnecessary, include:
  - Is this a new and improved version of something I already have?

- Do I really need the extra "bells and whistles"?

- What will I do with the old model?

- Is this a "single-purpose" item such as an egg poacher or hot-dog-bun warmer?

- Can some other item at home fulfill the same purpose?

- Take a careful look at "freebies"—three months of free magazines, for instance. Do you have time to read *Racing World, Hairstyle Hints,* and *Tofu Times* each month? Remember, time is money. Every free offer has a hidden "hook" too—after three months, that free magazine starts charging a subscription fee; the special trial offer membership of the auto club becomes a permanent fixture on your credit card unless it's canceled after the trial date.

- You could probably pave your driveway by now with free floppy disc and CD offers for Internet service. Review your Internet service contract every three months or so for any better offers; in between times, use the discs as Frisbees®.

- Make it a hard and fast rule that for every item of clothing you bring home, you remove an item from your closet. You will be amazed at how this not only keeps clutter from forming in your closet, but how your wardrobe will take on new life as you become more selective about the clothing you own. Many resale shops now offer consignment services that pay you in cash or trade for your clothing, so don't hesitate to make use of these stores if you don't wish to donate items to a charity. This also keeps impulse buying to a minimum.

• If you love to catalog shop, mark the page number of the item you plan to order on the front of the catalog. Wait two days and look at the item again. Generally the impulse to buy it is gone and you can trash the catalog. If not, then go ahead and order the item.

• While we're talking about impulse buying, here's a tip: When you're in one of those moods and you know a purchase is imminent, steer clear of trendy items that will lead to "buyer's remorse" before you even get home. Instead, select a basic item that fits with your current wardrobe. A white blouse or neutral-colored sweater will get a lot more use.

• Show your children the difference between a "looking day" and a "buying day." Malls and specialty stores are exciting places, full of new and unusual products, and looking is absolutely free. Think of these places as museums; they are full of interesting objects, but you don't have to own them to enjoy them. You can enjoy an hour or two in your local mall with the kids on a looking day, and end with an ice cream cone at the food court. Begin this habit early, and they won't beg and whine for every toy they see.

• Does your heart beat faster just thinking of your neighborhood warehouse store? A bargain isn't a bargain if you really don't need the item in the first place. Fourteen cans of tuna are not a great deal if you hate seafood, no matter what the price. If you must shop at a warehouse store, do so on a full stomach and with a list. When tempted to deviate from your list, promise yourself you'll try that item next time. This way, you're not denying yourself—just deferring the purchase for a little while. Try it—it works!

With a little practice, clutter control will become second nature to you. Not only will you reap the benefits of a more orderly, organized home, but you'll feel in control of your life and your finances too! Keeping your life simple is possible even in today's fast-paced world—and it's well worth the effort. As the Queen Mother often told me, "The best things in life are free." Good friends, a loving family, and a happy heart can't be bought—but there will be time to enjoy them when your life is well organized.

Resource Guide

Here I've compiled a comprehensive list of agencies and organizations that will gladly accept your donated clothing, appliances, furniture, computers, and even cars. There's even a special section on handling the sale of your collectibles.

Clothing, Household Goods, Furniture, and Appliances

Look in your Yellow Pages under "Clothes—Consignment and Retail" for a shop near you that accepts clothing in exchange for cash or credit.

You can donate your clothing, household goods, appliances, and furniture to any of the following organizations:

Salvation Army

1–800–95–TRUCK (87825)
The Salvation Army has thrift stores located throughout North America. Call to schedule a pickup from the store near you.

St. Vincent de Paul

A national organization with thrift stores throughout the country. Contact your local chapter to arrange a pickup. The phone number will be listed in the Yellow Pages under "Social Service Organizations."

American Council of the Blind

This agency has thrift stores in most metropolitan areas. Call 1-800-866-3242 to find a store nearest you. They will provide you with the local number to call for a pickup.

Red Cross

1-800-HELP NOW (435-7669)
This number is for clothing donations only.

Goodwill Industries

Go to *www.goodwill.org* for a list of locations near you, or contact them at:

Goodwill Industries
9200 Rockville Pike
Bethesda, MD 20814
1-301-530-6500

Computer Donations

Any of the above organizations will gladly accept your computer donations. Don't forget that your local hospital, trade school, or area charter schools are always in need of computers too, as well as your local school district. Look in the blue pages of your phone directory under "State Government— Department of Education" for further information.

Vehicle Donations

To donate your car, contact Vehicle Donation Processing Center, Inc., a national processing agent for charities seeking vehicles. Call 1-800-269-6814, or go to *www.charityfunding.com* on the internet. They are registered with the Better Business Bureau.

Collection Sale and Donations

Collections of coins, silver, or rare objects will be gladly accepted as donations by antiques dealers (and most family members!), but if you would prefer to sell your collection, try an on-line auction site. Here are the URLs of two:

www.ebay.com
www.ubid.com

For a comprehensive list of on-line auction sites, go to *www.internetauctionlist.com.*

To learn the value of your collection, visit your local antiques dealer, check with your public library for a current price guide, or go to *www.theappraisernetwork.com* on the Internet. At this site you can post a free appraisal request, read the most commonly asked questions, and get help preparing an appraisal request.